Rachael Nealis

D0559520

"Are you ready to believe and live like you mean it? Then come with James on this journey beyond belief and see what God will do. Your life of miracles may be right around the bend."

"*God.net* is real. James doesn't make happily-ever-after promises. He simply describes how listening to God works. Sometimes you get it right; sometimes you don't. Even if you hear from God, your dream still may die. No one saw more unhappy endings than the prophet Jeremiah, yet he could not resist God's voice. Jonah truly heard God, but the destruction he announced never came. Like the shaggy edges of real life, *God.net* wrestles with the ambiguities of keeping your faith fervent even when it is assaulted in deserts and by disappointments. That is why this book is both comforting and beneficial."

"*God.net* forced me to look in the mirror again. It challenged me to move past my selfish motivations and my embarrassing secrets and cling to the naked truth of the gospel. I often stink at being like Jesus, but James Langteaux has reminded me once again that believing is a daily process, a journey that begins and ends at the Cross."

GOD.NET

THE JOURNEY BEYOND BELIEF

JAMES ALEXANDER LANGTEAUX

Multnomah®Publishers *Sisters, Oregon*

GOD.NET
published by Multnomah Publishers, Inc.
© 2001 by James Langteaux

International Standard Book Number: 1-57673-990-2

Cover design by Christopher Gilbert,
Uttley DouPonce DesignWorks, Sisters, Oregon

Author jacket photos and interior photos by Kevin Rolly

Cover image by Photonica

Quotes from *The Alchemist* are from: Paulo Coelho and Alan R. Clarke, trans.,
The Alchemist (San Francisco: Harper San Francisco, 1993).

Scripture quotations are from:
The Holy Bible, New International Version © 1973, 1984
by International Bible Society, used by permission of Zondervan Publishing House

Also quoted:
The Holy Bible, New King James Version (NKJV) © 1984 by Thomas Nelson, Inc.

New American Standard Bible (NASB) © 1960, 1977 by the Lockman Foundation.

The Amplified Bible (AMP) © 1965, 1987 by Zondervan Publishing House.

The Amplified New Testament © 1958, 1987 by the Lockman Foundation.

Multnomah is a trademark of Multnomah Publishers, Inc.
and is registered in the U.S. Patent and Trademark Office.

The colophon is a trademark of Multnomah Publishers, Inc.

Printed in the United States of America

For information:
MULTNOMAH PUBLISHERS, INC.
POST OFFICE BOX 1720
SISTERS, OREGON 97759

Library of Congress Cataloging-in-Publication Data
Langteaux, James Alexnder.
  God.net / by James Alexander Langteaux.
     p.cm.
  ISBN 1-57673-990-2
  1. Evangelistic work. I. Title: God dot net. II. Title.
  BV3795 .L26 2001
  269'.2–dc21

                    2001003216

01 02 03 04 05—10 9 8 7 6 5 4 3 2 1 0

WHO PUT THE DeAd IN DEDICATION?

JESUS.

Jesus Himself said, "Greater love has no one than this, that he lay down his life for his friends." I have witnessed that sort of love, sacrifice, and dedication in the life of Jolene Jackson. Because she could see past "the here and now" and into "the there and then," at the most critical times she put her life on the line for me. She is so much more than a friend. I wouldn't be writing these words today if she had not risked so much at such great personal cost. She chose to believe when I could not.

Thank you, Jolene. This little book is dedicated to you.

WITH THANKS...

Where to begin?

First, a very special thank-you to my father. We've recently become the best of friends, and I don't have the words to express the gratitude and appreciation I have for this man of integrity—a man who read hard words in *God.com* and let me know that no matter where I've been and what I've done, he loves me. Those words have brought healing, light, and life…and a much richer understanding of the love of my Father God. Thanks, Dad. I love you too. (Love and thanks to his amazing wife, Jan, the woman who taught me how to ride a bike and tie my shoes. I'm still doing both today!)

To my mother and stepfather, who raised me and gave me the hope that I stand on. For their generosity, love, and belief in me—even when I lost the way. And man, can my mother pray. Thank you, Mom. (I'm alive today.) I love you both very much.

To my own private St. Jude—the greatest editor to walk the earth—Judith St. Pierre, a woman who writes like the wind, behaves like a saint, and laughs in the face of the storm. I cannot tell you how grateful I am for your love, your life, and your willingness to break out of the norm.

To the great cloud of friends and witnesses who have surrounded me during the year I'll simply call "Desert Storm." Thank you Marian, Diane and Graham, Norm and the good Dr. Linda, Brian, Weyman and Sue, Anthony and Julia, Cindy and Mike, Cathie (Ginge) and Dave, Chris and Karen, Matthew, the Aarons, David Pierce, Stu and Michelle, Jim and Stephanie, Bruce Wilkinson, John Hasbrouck, Still James, Adrienne, and Jerri. And to all my new friends who read *God.com* and took the time to write: Thank you for sharing with me a bit of your lives.

To my incredible family in the community of The Junction, where I'm walking out believe, and my pastor, workout partner, and friend, Terry Fouche, and his wife, Linda. (Thank you both for leaving your homeland to live in the land of believe.)

To Graham and his family in New Zealand for the laughter and music and for choosing to believe and live like you mean it, despite the hardships.

To Don Jacobson, a man I greatly love and admire. A very special thanks to you and the family at Multnomah for making this dream a reality. You are all loved beyond belief.

And mostly, thanks G.

FOREWORD

NORM MINTLE

It's cold. Rainy. Dreary. It's not at all what an almost-June day should be like, even in Chicago.

God.net is a book that takes you through the cold, rainy, dreary dark nights of James Alexander Langteaux's road trip with God.

I read his first book, *God.com,* and like thousands, I found myself marveling at the creative brilliance of my best friend's description of his journey with God and how he began to hear the voice of our almighty Father and translate it as a guide for the rest of us. I'd lived much of that journey with him. And I've lived much of *the rest of the story* that's in this book.

But although I'm still in awe of James's poetic prowess, I'm far more convinced that he has discovered truths about God that he had only glimpsed before.

You see, in the desert we die. And then we live.

A desert is a funny thing. You don't really realize you're in it until you've been there a while. There's never a flashing neon sign that says: "Welcome to the desert. Prepare to die." But, driven by the Holy Spirit, Jesus went into the desert to do just that.

In my own most recent desert, I didn't want to believe that

the Spirit of God had driven me into such an abyss. Deserts are quiet places only if you don't let the cries of encircling vultures get to you. I got very thirsty before I realized that there wasn't an oasis nearby.

My silence ended with an intense screaming session with God. Actually, I was the only one screaming. When I finally quieted down, I whispered a P.S.: *Oh, and if there's anything that's hindering my escape from this desert, please show me. Amen.*

That's the only part God heard—or at least answered.

Not everyone who is on a journey beyond belief has gone through a desert.

Not yet.

But you will, trust me.

Trust Him.

Use *God.net* as your travelogue. It will help get you through the driest—or wettest—ugliest darkness you've ever faced.

Norm Mintle

NORM MINTLE
Director, School of Cinema, Television and Theatre Arts,
Regent University

AN A.D.D. TRILOGY

A MOVEMENT IN 3 PARTS.

A MUSICAL JOURNEY TO BE LIVED IN THE KEY OF BE

This book is a nonlinear experience—
almost like three books for the price of one.

IF YOU'RE IN THE MOOD FOR A STORY, GO DIRECTLY TO PART 2.

FOR NAVIGATIONAL HELP ON YOUR JOURNEY, START
WHERE MOST PEOPLE DO.

IF YOU'D RATHER GO FISHING WITH ME, SKIP TO WHAT I HAVE
CLEVERLY CALLED PART 3.

WWW.GOD.NET

A WORLDWIDE WEB AND A GREAT BIG NET...TO BRING IN THE REST—

THE REST OF THE STORY,

THE REST OF HIS CHILDREN,

AND THE REST THAT COMES WHEN YOU REALLY DO

believe.

THE REST OF THE STORY

WHERE ARE YOU NOW?

Through hundreds of e-mails, readers of *God.com* have asked me this question in a thousand different ways. "Are you still struggling?" "How are you handling the battle?" "What can I do? I'm married and I still feel gay." "I read your book and was blown away. Now three weeks later I'm right back in the middle of my old madness, and I don't know what to say!"

I think I know what to say:

WELCOME TO THE DESERT OF THE REAL.

God.com called the reader to join a revolution—it was *Braveheart* meets *Dr. Seuss.* But no matter how much we've cried or how our lives have felt shaken, not stirred, by words we've read or things we've heard, just on the other side of believe we will all find ourselves in the desert of the real.

IT IS REAL. And *real life* is a lot different than *the real world.* Real life has no commercial breaks, and our house is never quite as cool or situated in as chic a spot. Our circle of friends may not always have the one gay character, the rebel, the model, and the hapless victim; our clothes may not be as hip; our jobs may be a little less than lackluster. But at least our life is real. You are real and God is real. And in the desert of the real we can keep on telling the truth to one another and be honest about how we feel.

THAT IS MY OASIS.

What would happen if we really told the truth? At least most of it most of the time? I know for having told it once how grateful you can be. Many of you have thanked me for my transparency and congratulated me for having dealt courageously with topics that are considered dangerous in today's society.

But was that all there was to it? Was all of that just a drive-by truthing, leaving me to live amid accolades for that one telling of a tough truth? If that's the case, I wish I'd never done it, because the point of telling you my story, or at least a lyrical condensation of it, was to open us up to more truth.

In telling the truth we can find freedom in vulnerability, but we can also assume a false sense of responsibility. In that vulnerable pose, we realize that the world is now looking and that it actually knows what to look for, so we begin to *act* like we have our act together to uphold the power of our message.

TRUE OR FALSE DOCTRINE?

But it isn't our job to uphold the power of our message. It isn't even *our* message—it's His message—and He put the power in it, so it's up to Him to dazzle with the results. It can't be up to you or me. Our job is simply to believe and live like we mean it.

Just don't be surprised if you find yourself in a mess after making bold proclamations about your progress. The other team is not going to sit idly by and watch you run toward the goal without some serious interference. It may get so serious that you question whether you ever really had an experience with this interactive God.

To tell you the truth, after *God.com* hit the shelves and the sales took off and the e-mails began pouring in, I began to notice a quietness involving the things of Him. Suddenly I couldn't recognize His voice. I was talking on radio programs about getting away with God and allowing time for Him to speak. But my time with Him was becoming less and less, and my self-proclaimed ability to hear His voice was becoming more and more of a mess. I became less inclined to speak about the God I claimed would speak when He grew silent and my bucket of faith began to leak. Truth be told, I went through a long dry spell. It was a very real desert, but I've lived to tell—

THE TRUTH.

In *God.net* I want to tell you the truth of my story, and I want to tell you the truth about God, and the only way I can really tell you His story is to tell you my story because my story has now merged with His. I want to tell you of the mountains and the valleys, because as high as the mountain highs can get, there often seem to be a lot more valleys so low. SOLO. And the journey can seem way too long for the number of rest stops you find along the road.

If you've taken the bold leap of believe, you'll know exactly what I mean. The adrenaline races and the poetry of revolution stirs the batter of your soul, but when the bullets begin to fly, you see the hell this war can hold.

THIS IS NOT A GAME!

It's a battle, and there's a very real enemy who doesn't like you much. But don't worry, it isn't about you—it's about the One you serve. Because Jesus said, "If the world hates you, keep in mind that it hated me first. No servant is greater than his master." Now with the Internet, cable, and digital television, it seems that the hate just spreads so much faster.

To survive, you need God, you need His Spirit, and you need His power working in and through. You need to let go of your preconceptions about what you need to do. You need to ask and go looking through His authoritative Word for the things that will equip you when the battle seems absurd.

And you really do need friends. Friends who are empowered by the same Spirit that raised Christ from the dead. Friends who are part of your network in a community of believe. You need to embrace honesty and transparency, because to live in freedom, we are required to confess our sins—not just to God alone, but to one another—for His real power of deliverance to kick in. (And not just once, but over and over again.) There's so much more that He can do if you will only fall recklessly and wildly into His arms of protection and into His great and saving NET. THE GOD-NET.

I know that many might fear to follow a God who leaves so many questions unanswered on a journey this tough. But there is HOPE. I know it for a fact because I drive by it every week. On my way to teach and learn at the university, I ride my motorcycle past a sign that says:

CITY OF HOPE
NEXT 2 EXITS.

And every time I pass that sign, the road ahead looks a little less daunting.

So as we travel through the desert of the real, I'll be sending POSTCARDS FROM THE EDGE OF HOPE, because without hope, people perish, and I'm sick of seeing so much disease, decay, and death.

Though you'll be tempted, tried, and tested, there's hope. I want to remind you that you are not alone and help make the desert stretches feel a bit less daunting and a little more like home. If you can grow comfortable outside of comfort, it will be Jesus that you see—the Jesus who was and is a real revolutionary.

His was a cry for life. But the life He promised all of us is not a life that is free of strife. We learn in the times of battle; we are honed in the deserts, hot and real. And if we can learn to believe past what we see and if we can trust less and less how we feel, then and only then will we move toward the rest—the rest of what He has in mind when we move beyond what we can see. And it is rest that He desires for us—that rest that comes when we finally do believe.

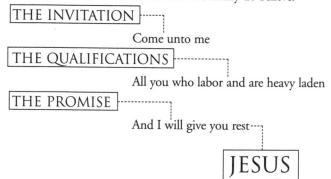

So *God.net* is the rest of the story. That's what I want to share with you—the rest of my story and the rest that God intends for us to live in when we believe His story.

But *God.net* is also a fish story. Most fish stories are hard to believe, but Jesus asked each one of us to move beyond belief and take up our nets and become fishers of men.

As you learn to cast your net and tell your story, you'll see blind eyes opened to the truth—the truth of a God who never fails. If ours is a God who truly speaks, it should be our job to move inside belief and begin to hear words of hope and life and promise for the strangers that we meet.

Hitchhikers on this journey will have a hard time ignoring you and the God you claim to know if you share things from His heart to theirs—things you can never know without

DEEP SEE FISHING IN A CYBER SORT OF SEA.

At the end of our journey, all we'll really have are our stories—stories we must share with one another around the great, flickering fire circle. What will your story be? What tale will you ultimately have to tell? Will your journey lead to paradise, or will it lead to hell? You are the author of your story—the traveler on your journey. But you are not alone. There's a company of friends on this journey beyond belief—friends who are learning to love and trust and walk together as fishermen of men.

This road trip begins with a few very small, but important steps. The first step may be to ask for the willingness to move, or perhaps just the willingness to hear. Maybe yours is simply to ask God to remove all of your fear. Fear and doubt are robbing us of the joy and excitement our God intends, and we can either sit out on the sidelines or make this God our friend. I believe that He is the greatest friend we could ever come to know. I believe that if we are willing to listen and obey, we'll hear this friend yell, "GO!"

If you want to turn your life into an adventure and take a journey beyond belief, I invite you to pick up this book and let its words wash over you as you make Jesus your best friend—the One who died for you and the One who is dying to be with you on a trip that never really ends.

PART- I

WELCOME TO THE DESERT OF THE REAL

A SURVIVAL GUIDE FOR LIFE ON THE BACK SIDE OF BELIEVE

Despite the claims I've made, there are times when our interactive God just doesn't seem to speak, and our cry for *Revolution* can grow a little weak. That's not at all unusual when you venture boldly into the desert on the back side of believe. In times like that, you'll need to know how to survive and thrive as you make your own journey from the mountain through the desert and finally to the **See** (that amazing land where your eyes are finally opened and you see what Jesus sees).

So here are some basic road rules and travel tips:

When you find yourself in the desert, be sure you eat the right food, read the guide Book, and look to your Guide with Transparen**See**. He will help you when you feel like giving up or giving in. All you really need to do is ask and act. And now more than ever, you'll need some trusted friends, to surround you like a net while they pray with you and help protect you from sandstorms, false dogs and idols, and swarms of dancing fleas.

If all of this sounds easy, read on, please....

BACK IN THE DAYS
WHEN GOD WOULD
SPEAK...

IN THE BEGINNING WAS THE WORD, AND
THE W O R D WAS WITH GOD

(Maybe that's why I couldn't hear it.)

We are dying to hear God's voice, and we are dying because we don't. Not hearing is especially frustrating if you read a book that claims you'll hear Him if you're willing to believe and take the time to listen. Books like that can convince you to give peace a chance, so you turn off everything and listen for His voice for a few minutes, hours, or even days. But even though you thought you believed, you end up hearing nothing at all, and the silence leads to angst, as you wonder why God didn't take the time to call.

I EVEN HAVE CALL W A I T I N G ...

It's bad enough when that happens, but imagine writing a book that makes that sort of claim, only to find that shortly after it

hits the shelves and begins to sell, the voice that had been so clear
has somehow disappeared. And the guy who claims to have cor-
nered the market on hearing God's voice is suddenly faced with a
choice: to let go of the crazy notion that God will speak, or choose
instead to continue to believe—and to speak, even when God
doesn't.

I have to admit: **I found it so much easier to believe back
in the days when God would speak...**

It wasn't so long ago. One morning my phone rang while I
was shaving in my loft on a rooftop in downtown Los Angeles. It
was Multnomah Publishers calling—a wrong number of sorts.
Before the woman could finish apologizing, I asked if she would
transfer me to the voice mail of someone in marketing. I had a
great idea I wanted to pass along. (I think I have great ideas about
three hundred times a day.)

My random message led to a meeting with the VP of marketing. Jeff was gracious and direct. I had a video concept, but he
wasn't all that impressed and suggested that I kill that particular
dream. "I'm excited about how you hear from God, though," he
said, "and I wonder if you could get a book proposal on my desk
as soon as possible."

Despite the fact that I had been dreaming of being an author
since I was seven or eight years old, I had a video idea, and a book

was out of the question. My boss at the video production house where I worked said that if I landed a book deal (he paid for me to visit Jeff in Nashville), he would have to kill me. "THIS WILL ONLY BE ANOTHER DISTRACTION FOR YOU, POSTER BOY FOR A.D.D."

A strange mix of emotions overwhelmed me as I flew home from that meeting. I decided to give it all over to God and let Him lead if this was meant to be. While flying forward at nearly six hundred miles per hour, I fell backward in my seat and landed in that otherworldly place where reality floats between the waking world and dreams. And suddenly it was as if God Himself spoke, giving the title and concept to me.

"GOD.COM: BECOME INTERACTIVE WITH THE GOD OF THE UNIVERSE. LOG ON TO HIS PAGE AND YOUR SOFTWHERE WILL DRAMATICALLY CHANGE WHEREVER YOU GO."

I sat bolt upright, and my pen could barely keep up with the God-flow. Every chapter title poured out in a flood, along with short paragraphs that captured the essence of each one. I was convinced that this was a God-thing because only moments before I hadn't had the vaguest idea of what this book should accomplish or what the title should be. This was a miracle, if you ask me.

Those were the days when God was speaking in torrents. I remember the excitement that filled the air after the book proposal reached Don, the president of Multnomah. The waiting was excruciating. Finally, God told me the exact day and hour that Don would call to discuss the project.

"Hey, God told me the president is going to call at 2 P.M. today," I told everyone in the office. "Please don't disturb us!"

Everyone chuckled at my bold and childlike belief, but I sat expectantly by the phone. It rang at 2:07, and when I answered and heard Don's voice, I burst into laughter—a very strange introduction to a man I hadn't met yet.

"I'm laughing because God told me you'd be calling at two," I explained. "You're late."

I loved Don's reply: "If you really believed, you would have answered the phone, 'Hello, Don.'"

As we firmed up a deal on the publishing agreement, God did it again. He said that Don would be calling at ten on Tuesday. I waited. No call. Then I realized that God hadn't said which Tuesday. The following week, when my phone rang at 10:03 on Tuesday, I answered boldly, **"Hello, Don."**

"Uh…I'm not Don. This is Michael in Philly."

I blushed, apologized, and asked Michael to hold while I grabbed the other line.

"Hello, this is James."

"Don Jacobson here." I thought I would cry.

AN A.D.D. AXIOM

[Hearing from God is not an exact science.]

I explained what had happened, and we both had a good laugh.

Finally, the time came for me to fly to meet the publisher face-to-face. As we flew over Oregon, I heard over and over again in my head, *I'm giving you the land. I'm giving you the land.* As beautiful as the land appeared, I couldn't figure out what I was going to do with Oregon.

I even called my friend Jolene back at the office to tell her what had happened. "God told me that He is giving me the land."

"What land? Oregon?" She sounded kind of busy.

"I guess. God kept saying it over and over. I just don't know.... But you sound pretty busy, so I probably should let you go."

I waited nervously in front of the tiny airport for Don to arrive. I don't know if I imagined this, but when he drove up in his Suburban, he seemed a bit surprised. I later learned that no potential author had ever shown up wearing a T-shirt, earrings, and jeans—not to mention a leather motorcycle jacket with the German word for *crazy* written on the sleeves.

I could tell that we were both unsettled about having lunch together. I could barely read the menu, much less decide what to eat. Finally, Don broke the ice by telling me his own story of believe, and I began to feel a bit more normal, like I could finally breathe. But just when Don reached the most dramatic part of his story—where he lay bleeding and dying in the woods—God's words again interrupted my thoughts: *"I'm giving him the land. I'm giving him the land."* I had no idea what that meant. What if he didn't want "the land"? But I knew that God was more interested in my obeying than in my understanding what it was all about. So I interrupted Don to tell him what God was shouting in my head.

SOME A.D.D. ADVICE

Admitting to hearing voices in your head usually won't help you secure a major book deal.

Don looked extremely surprised, and I felt like a complete idiot. But it turned out that the only need Multnomah had at that time was for fifty or so acres of land for a new campus. But, Don explained, getting it was almost impossible because nearly all the land in Sisters is federally protected. It looked as if he would have to move the company and all the employees too. A major hassle.

But after that strange interruption, Don decided to believe. I don't know what has come of that. Since then, there were times when land became available, but then the situation changed again. All I know is that they haven't moved, because I keep mailing things to the same address. The point is that, circumstances aside, God just wants us to believe.

I know for a fact that God will speak because He says throughout His Word that He does and He will. But I miss those days when God was speaking in miraculous sorts of ways. Life seemed so much easier back then, when God seemed to be breathing exceptionally hard.

What I had to learn is that there may be long periods of time when He doesn't speak. Then it doesn't take long for the other team to convince us that we imagined it all. Elijah once experienced an amazing pyrotechnic display when God sent fire from heaven to consume the unbelief of a wavering nation. Still, it wasn't long until that prophet's faith went on vacation. Right after that miraculous firestorm from heaven, which proved the very power and might of the one true God, Elijah found himself right smack in the middle of the desert of the real. There in the shadow of his doubt and a silly little tree, ELIJAH HAD ONE REQUEST:

"GOD, PLEASE JUST ANNIHILATE ME!

Coming as it did on the heels of one of the most spectacular events of all time, Elijah's experience proves that it doesn't matter who you are—you can be a prophet of the ages or just a regular guy like me—if you move out into the dark land of believe, it will only be a matter of time until you find that you're deceived by looming clouds that gather after miracles reveal. This, my friends, is a battle for the truth; it's not about how we feel. It takes even more belief to hold on when the things that started out so great now look extremely bleak.

I'm saying all of this because I've just come out of a very intense time of silence. I could not hear God speak, and the words I thought He was speaking were more often coming from me. I couldn't figure out what was going on. The more days that passed, the more panic-stricken I became. I was wondering what had happened to the God who I've claimed will speak—the God who doesn't change. Was He mocking me?

THEN I WOKE UP.

The mockery had come from me. In the midst of speaking on radio and TV about the virtues of going on-line with an inter-active God, I found that I'd grown complacent about some of the things He was asking of me. My God had told me that He wanted to spend time with me. Somehow I thought that my writing and speaking and sharing would do. But the few moments I gave to Him alone weren't enough, and He began to make Himself very clear.

BY HIS SILENCE.

And the silence wasn't the worst of it. I could fix that by sur-
rounding myself with more people, activities, and events. I could
fill the dead air with my favorite music or even by speaking profoundly and authoritatively about God with radio hosts and my
good friends. But somehow I missed the point that my very best
friend was now on hold while I spent time with my homies and
left Him out in the cold.

That was not a good thing. The chaos and distraction I welcomed into my life brought confusion and double-mindedness to
all of my ways. I hate to admit this. I thought that somehow I had
arrived at a powerfully unique place: I had God on my leash and
could ask Him to sit and show others how He would speak on
command. But the power I tried to leash belongs to the Spirit that
runs free—to the Most High God, who rules eternally.

Finally I came to my senses. I stood still amid the madness
I'd embraced to drown out the silence of the God who had turned
His face. I stopped and asked myself what was the last thing I
remembered Him asking me to do—the last thing I had chosen
not to do—and if that could be what was keeping Him from
speaking to me, hanging with me, directing me. I had a very real
choice. I could hold on to life as I had grown accustomed to it, or
I could go back to a command that had turned out to be very

uncomfortable: "Go up to the mountain and be alone with Me."

Now being alone seemed even more frightening. Now I was so much farther from those times of intimacy because I had moved so far from Him and was clinging that much harder to my close friends. How could I let go now and trust that I would not be left alone in the cleft of the rock in a pile of dust? Whom was I to trust?

NO VOICE. NO CHOICE.

In the end, it was an easy decision. My life had grown so confusing that I could feel nothing but my hardened heart, see nothing but my false gods, and hear nothing but my own jumbled thoughts. I was making stupid decisions, and I was paying a ridiculously high cost.

Part of that cost involved leaving my home church. I had felt that somehow in God's silence I had been left in the lurch. I figured there must be something wrong in that community of believers, a place where God should clearly speak. But for the life of me, I couldn't hear Him, so I decided that it was time to leave. What a terrible mistake.

REWIND

So I went back and undid all the decisions I could possibly reverse from the time I stepped out of God's presence and into the curse. I asked my church family to forgive me for blaming them

for my hearing problem and told my friends that I had to step
away from all of them for a season. I thought it might be for just a
few days, but it ended up being for several weeks as clarity replaced
the haze.

In walking away from that terrible place where God was
silent, I've asked some important questions—like, "What went
wrong?" And I'm learning some invaluable things, one of which is
that God is a jealous lover. He will still be full of grace and love,
but there will be a price to pay if we allow our love to grow cold.

"I know your deeds, that you are neither cold nor hot. I wish you were
either one or the other! So, because you are lukewarm—neither hot
nor cold—I am about to spit you out of my mouth."

WWW.REVELATION@3.15–16.NET

Rather than end up as God's spit, I decided that I had to go
back to the last word I remembered Him saying—the last word
before I stopped hearing anything. And I had to search His authoritative Word to determine what had brought on the deafening
silence that led to alienation and confusion.

THE LAST WORD

"If you abide in My word, you are My disciples indeed."

WWW.JOHN@8.31.NET/NKJV

Jesus said, "My sheep hear my voice." That must mean He does in fact speak. He said so Himself, if you are willing to believe. But there's something even more important than hearing from God through a voice in your head, because at times there is so much noise around us that there's no voice at all.

There's a safety net that God Himself put in place thousands of years ago. It's the net of His Word, written down for all to see, often in a leather-bound black book, a book we all should read. Some claim that the only true version is the King James, but it's really a matter of your own personal taste. That version, set down in the parlance of Shakespeare, is beautifully written, but for some it's a bit tough to swallow. There are other translations I find more accessible and far easier to follow.

More important than the version, though, is that we take the time to taste—to see for ourself what the Most High God of the universe has done, to meditate, and to drink in the words of His Son. Because if we really do want to hear God's voice, we need something authentic to hold up to the other words we think He may have spoken. If we don't look into a true mirror, it will forsooth be nigh unto impossible (a King James moment) for us to see the counterfeit in the sea of words.

THE SEE OF WORDS.

We clearly see in God's authoritative Word that the disobedient receive their just punishment. And sometimes the worst punishment is just knowing that God has left and that we will never enter His rest, leaving us in a land of constant worry, doubt, and stress.

> Now with whom was He angry forty years? Was it not with those who sinned, whose corpses fell in the wilderness? And to whom did He swear that they would not enter His rest, but to those who did not obey?

WWW.HEBREWS@3.17–18.NET/NKJV

Disobedience was the first problem that led me to that place of silence, separation, and distraction. Quite honestly, it felt a lot like death. During the final days of my stay in the loft in downtown L.A., God had made it perfectly clear to me that He wanted to take me to the mountain to spend time with Him in the cleft of the rock. It sounded amazing—on paper. But as I transitioned to a little

tree house, built in an actual cleft of the rock in a quaint and magi-
cal canyon just east of Los Angeles, I found that I had grown very
accustomed to the nonstop activity of life in the city. I had a great
roommate and a collection of interesting friends who would pop in
and out of my life on a regular basis—not to mention the rooftop
church that gathered there under (and above) the stars on Sunday
nights.

But this was to be a new time of **REST**—the rest that comes
when we really do believe and then live beyond belief in the center
of His love, in quiet and in calm. God had spoken powerfully to
me through about three hundred close friends who are even closer
to God than they are to me. In one big, unified voice, they all said,
"This is a time of rest and intimacy with God. Go up to the
mountain and listen and be."

So I made the move to that amazingly peaceful place, where
huge decks, giant shade trees, and the sheer enchantment of the
place cried out, "Rest! Be with the One who created the beauty
you see." I tried.

BUT LIKE ANY ADDICT, I NEEDED A FIX. AND I NEEDED IT NOW.

When I got to the mountain, I just wanted to scream. The
silence was too much. The idea of God showing up in such a quiet

place seemed so foreign, and resting in peace felt like dying to me.

I don't know why, because in the past I'd spent a lot of time alone listening and writing in very quiet cabins. I even remember thinking, *I wish God would give me a place like this where I can write another book.* He did, but by that time I'd become addicted to too many distractions and had forgotten what it felt like to be alone with Him. I prayed a lot with my friends, but I think that joining a friend in prayer or praying in a group—as good as it is—is nothing like that intimate time alone with the One you really love.

My disobedience had to be painful to Him, because in retrospect I see how much pain I inflicted on myself and on my friends by my inability to follow His lead and lean into Him. My disobedience caused me to lean into them instead of Him, and although these friendships were a gift from God, I believe that I took that gift and turned it into another, competing god. Somehow, in my fear of being alone in a very quiet place, I elevated these little gods to God's rightful place.

JESUS HAS LEFT THE BUILDING.

Disobedience leads to God's disappearance. I know all about "He will never leave us or forsake us," but when we are disobedient, He simply can't be present like He is when we're in a relationship of obedience born of love. I don't know about you, but for me, God's absence leads to huge distractions. As soon as I sensed the lack of

God's presence, I started to embrace every possible diversion—people, things, events—anything at all that could fill that God-shaped void. I was very successful. I filled my time with all sorts of unnecessary things. I found myself in a state of confusion with a sense of being spun out of control. Even many of my good friends could see a crazy look in my darting eyes.

I, however, could have sworn that I was fine.

I've learned a few things as I've tried to sort this out. Disobedience leads to God's silence. Emptiness leads to distraction. Distraction leads to darkness. Because once we know what it's like to feel the presence of the living God, we try to fill the void of His absence with things—darker and darker, hedonistic sorts of things. At least I know I do.

A GOD-SHAPED VOID IN STUPID 3-D:
DISOBEDIENCE,
DISTRACTION,
DARKNESS.

Jesus said that when we allow even a little darkness in through the eye-gate of the soul, we are going to become dark—not just in part, but dark in the whole. When we push God to the side, all sorts of other things become attractive. We may not choose to stare directly at evil, but we'll be willing to take stolen, sidelong glances.

And you know what? That's no different from drinking it all in or wallowing in the middle of a sick and desperate sin. Jesus said that whatever you allow yourself to think is pretty much what you will be, because out of the abundance of the heart our (sometimes filthy) mouths will speak.

But we have not been called to live in the land of the vile and obscene. We have been called to live lives that are obedient and clean. I just hadn't figured out how to live in that place for long periods of time. For a while, others could clearly see His light shine in me, but with just enough distance or absence or time on my own, it wasn't long before I was back on the throne. And that, my friend, is the problem.

MAN WAS NOT MEANT TO BE ALONE OR ON THE THRONE

At least not apart from Him. Because the natural desire of a heart apart from God is desperately wicked, and, really, no one can know it. When we give ourselves any sort of credit—thinking that somehow we are immune to dark and consuming things—it won't be long before we find ourselves totally ruined.

SIN IS DESPERATELY DECEITFUL AND DIABOLICALLY DESIGNED TO TAKE US ALL DOWN.

Disobedience leads to distraction, and distraction can take

us into darkness in any number of ways. If any of those ways involve sinful images on satellite, cable, or the Internet, we are allowing that darkness to snuff out the light in our souls.

The longer I live, the more surprised I am at how many who claim to be followers of Jesus are allowing the most heinous of things to pass through the windows of their souls. If we are completely honest with ourselves, we'll realize that the bulk of films we watch are full of vile and obnoxious things—things that would have been offensive to nearly all audiences not even twenty-five years ago. What has happened to us? How have we allowed ourselves to embrace so much darkness and yet feel absolutely no guilt, remorse, or shame? Jesus made no bones about it. He will not hang out where there is darkness and sin. God won't tolerate our taking it in. Because what we see is eventually what we become.

AS WE SEE, SO SHALL WE BE.

I know I sound old-fashioned, but there's no time for fashion when the world is spiraling so wildly out of control. And there's more at stake than just our single soul. There are the souls of all the people we meet—all those we encounter, to whom we should speak—and if we aren't full of His light and filled with His love, the words we have for them will be uninspired, unimpressive, and unbelievably cold. God's authoritative Word says so.

"Because of the increase of wickedness,
the love of most will grow cold."

WWW.MATTHEW@24.12.NET

God is not looking for people who are holier-than-thou, but for those who are trying like crazy to be more like Him. And really, I think that only a part of the struggle involves trying; most of the battle is all about dying—all about realizing that we are powerless apart from the power of God. When we come to that place, we can lay down our man-made holiness and in our very real and honest weakness look to Him to make us strong. In our weakness, He makes us strong. When we let Him. When we ask Him.

There's a fine line here. Someone may read this and think I'm saying that we have no power at all over sin. I'm not. We all must make ongoing decisions to avoid certain places, circumstances, and people—based on our levels of personal depravity, the history of our sin nature, and our very present need.

But our flesh is weak, and if we think that we can somehow do this in our own strength without Him, we are just being religious and deceived. When we try to make ourselves look holy, when we try to convince the world that we can do this on our own by following a bunch of rules, we might as well go home. That's a game none of us needs to play. Because we won't be able to keep it up. And even if we do, it's only on the outside, which makes us hypocrites of the very worst kind.

We must acknowledge our real, repetitive, ongoing sin. We must not allow the fact that we are dealing with the same thing over and over to keep us from falling back on our knees to ask Him to forgive us…AGAIN.

He will forgive us every single time we ask, every single time we need. And this God called Jesus does it willingly—or it would have been pointless for Him to bleed. His shed blood washes us clean. It has nothing to do with how good we can seem.

I also think we must have a network of friends with whom we can be brutally honest about our plight. We can't be too ashamed or too proud to admit to them that we have a desperate need— that we've stumbled or sinned or stepped into darkness instead of walking in the light. God loves us too much to allow us to continue under the weight of sin and the bondage that we enter in when we move into disobedience. If we humble ourselves and call on one another to pray powerfully and authoritatively over our sin and our shame, we will see the chains broken when we use the name above all names: JESUS.

As for me, when I decided to obey, I found myself reentering a place I had forgotten, a place I longed for and loved, one that I shared with my Creator and used to call home. The silent, lonely place was again filled with the very real voice and the very real love of my very real God. And it was incredible to feel the very real love of my family when I returned to my church. There was no judgment and not even one "I told you so," though many claimed to have known that I'd be back. When I did my prodigal-like return, my life in that community of believers—that network of friends—literally exploded. Forgiveness is such an incredible gift. Walking back into His presence and His power will give our spirit that needed lift.

Those of you who have experienced the very real and palpable presence of a very present and tangible God will know what I mean. If you have somehow moved away from that place, you will also know how real the craziness can seem. But there is so much grace on this road trip with God. There is so much love and for-giveness, even when we choose to go the wrong way. It says so in His authoritative Word. And for that, I'm truly glad.

OBEDIENCE BORN OF LOVE.

But there's something else I need to say: As we love Him, we will begin to obey Him—in a more mature sort of way—and obe-dience born of love will help us rise above the junk that tries to keep us all enslaved, be it gossip, gluttony, gayness, or greed. It's all sin—all born out of depravity, brokenness, desperation, and need. We all need; we all have hungers and cravings. The important thing is to feed on God's Word so we know what we should and should not eat.

JESUS AND JUNK FOOD

A Hunger for the Truth

3

EAT RIGHT. TRAVEL LIGHT. ANGEL FOOD AND DESERT FARE...

An old Indian proverb goes something like this:

A man asked a wise sage why he always seemed to make the wrong choices. Even though he knew what was right, he chose to do what was wrong. The old sage looked at him and replied, "My son, there are two dogs inside you, a black dog and a white dog. One is good and one is evil. They are constantly at war with each other, fighting to the death. "Which one is going to win?" asked the tormented man. "The one you feed," the wise man replied.

Food is so important on the journey beyond belief. Battles are won and lost depending on what we choose to ingest. Even on the other side of major victories, we can find ourselves on the dark side of the desert where the enemy will try to rob us of our life and joy and strength. If we haven't chosen the right nutrients to carry us through those desert times, we may find ourselves emaciated and helpless, or hopeless and fat—depending on what we've chosen to put in our travel packs. As for me, I'M FAT.

Not so much on the outside anymore, but a bit deeper down inside.

No matter what I see in the mirror—no matter how many months I spend training, snowboarding, or how low my body fat percentage may be—I still see a fat boy in the marred reflection of my mind's mirror. When you are wounded young, especially in those formative years, the image you have of yourself may end up far from reality.

WHAT YOU SEE IS WHAT YOU FEEL.

Alcoholics Anonymous discovered that powerful truth—and the power in the telling of truth—a long time ago. Although Christians tend not to take advice readily from "drunks," I think these broken friends have learned something that could help us all, if we are willing to tell the truth. Their secret is simply that they have no secrets.

At every meeting, members introduce themselves not by listing their accolades or degrees, but by telling one another how alcohol brought them to their knees.

"Hi, I'm Mike, and I'm an alcoholic."

"Hi, Mike," the group responds, and love just fills the room. Even if Mike hasn't had a drink in twenty-six years, he still owns the fact that he had a craving inside that drove him to drink far too many beers.

This gathering of the broken is honest. They don't put on airs, and they tell it like it is. In the telling they find freedom, accountability, and solace for the journey. And the journey leads to healing and healing leads to whole.

So—hi, I'm James.

AND I'M FAT.

It's a funny thing, being fat. You can't really put your finger on the day it happened. You don't even notice it yourself at first. What happens is that you start to hear people laugh when you pass them in the hall. They say things under their breath, and as time goes on they tend to get a little bit bolder. Meaner, maybe.

Finally a kid in the hall comes right out and says it.

HEY, FATSO!

He could follow that introduction with any number of things, but the pain of hearing those words numbs you to whatever insults follow. You stand there dripping in shame.

After a short season of disgrace, in which the word *fatso* is flung in your face, you start to look to people you love to confirm the fact that you really aren't.

"No, son, you are not fat. You're husky. You take after your mother's side of the family. They're all big boned." (That usually doesn't help, because no matter how big their bones may be, they all look fat to me.)

After a time of finding comfort in the kind words of your family and your very closest friends, you venture to a mirror—naked. It's a horrifying thing. There in the harsh, unfiltered light of the bathroom, you finally see it. You really are fat. And for the life of you, you can't remember when it happened. It just seemed to spring up from nowhere—a full-blown fat attack.

WHAT'S UP WITH FAT?

As obvious as this may seem, we're fat because we're hungry. We have a need. But instead of heading to the health-food aisle in the grocery store, we stop at the junk-food display for Oreos®, Twinkies®, Ding Dongs®, and more. We go for what's quick, convenient, and cheap. (Or at least we think so at the time.)

We all want to fill our need in the fastest way we can. I mean, when we're hungry, we want to eat *right now*. We don't want to have to go to the store, cut chicken and vegetables, sauté it all in olive oil, and serve it over rice. That may not even sound good to many of you. (But it really is very filling. I had some just last night.)

We want satisfaction and we want it now. I want to reach right out and grab a bag of Doritos® and let those deep-fried chips of corn dance deliriously across my taste buds as they make their way seductively to my growling, growing stomach.

I don't know if many of you are willing to admit to any of this. This hunger, I mean. I'm not even sure I should say these words, but I'm going to take the risk. I have little left to lose. Many of us are addicts with crazy cravings and a hunger we just can't seem to fill. Secretly, we're fat. Although we might not wear it on the outside, God sees it. And I think it makes Him sad.

Let's be honest. Many of us wait until it's too late to meet our needs in any other way. We wait so long that no one can see it and say, "There really is a better way." There in the hollow of our hunger we start our spiral down. And in the hollow of our hunger, it's not long before we drown.

BOOT UP.
LOG ON.
FALL IN
—SIN.

There in the darkness of your secret you pass a parade of junk food before your craving eyes. It may not even be intentional at first. You sit down to do some work and realize that research couldn't hurt. So you log on.

In a minute your mind wanders—it may just be your hunger propelling you—but you think of an interesting word. Hmm…I wonder what sort of web site this is?

So you type: WWW.BURGERLAND.COM.

HIT GO.

And away you go. That's all it takes. In the very first pop-up window is a juicy, airbrushed, professionally photographed piece of meat. Right there on the screen. How easy was that? There's no more time to think. Now you're hitting the Xs with frantic strokes like you're playing that gopher-pounding game at the carnival. You hit the *x,* and another pops up somewhere on your screen. The sickness seeps in, but you tell yourself that you're actually trying to stop the madness by minimizing the images and the guilt— which just brings on more images and more guilt. You're addicted. You know it, but for the moment, you just don't care.

Finally, after indulging in a fruitless frenzy of lusty images of every perverse form of pastry, poultry, and meat, you've had too much. But you can never get enough. So you carefully clean up your history and crawl between cold and guilty sheets.

Dear God, I am so sorry. I will never, ever do that again. You promised in Your Word that You would forgive me, and I promise I will not repeat my sin.

God keeps His promise, even though He knows that you won't keep yours.

YOU CAN'T KEEP YOURS.

And as you fall into a desperate, hungry sleep, you realize that this was round 995,463.

How many of us are willing to admit to being part of a scenario like the one I've just described? You know the cycle all too well. You fear the hunger even more than you fear spending an eternity in hell. But guess what? All of us are hungry, and we all have a need. It's how we choose to meet it and what that then will mean.

Internet junk food can never meet your need. It just makes you feel better that you haven't done the dirty deed. The meat stayed on the screen. But the funny thing is that Jesus said if you look upon a sandwich and taste it in your mind, it really is the same as eating it right out on the street. Isn't that bizarre? No one will know you are fat if you consume it only on a screen. No one but Jesus, that is; and for the most part, He's discreet.

But you are fat. You are addicted. And I don't care the brand of your bondage; like me, you have a hunger and a need.

My hunger was for love. I wanted the love that comes from a father's embrace—from a father I thought I never could have. So I listened to the snickers that started in the halls of my hell—a place I think we now call middle school—and then suddenly the laughter turned mean.

HEY, FAGGOT!

The adrenaline raced as the blood rushed through my veins. All I wanted to do was to cry and tell the dad I didn't know just how bad this hell could be. Just how hollow hell could feel. So I cried alone as I started my search to find someone or something to meet that father need. I was looking for a place to feed. Like I said before, when you're hungry, you do what's easy. You go to a place where people love you just the way you are—a place where they want you to believe that you are, in fact, a star. (Why is that place almost never a church and almost always a bar?) But once you've gone a bit too far in, it seems there's no choice but to embrace more sin.

I've been around the block, and I've been around the world, and I can see that many of you are fat—just like me. You've been hungry, and you're dying inside. Your hunger may be different than the one I've described; but the brand of junk food you have chosen to view, buy, or eat has caused you—like it did me—to lose a whole lot of sleep.

But you just can't help it. You've been raised in the church, and you know how bad this all seems, yet also how trapped we all seem. So you keep your secret safe, while you continue to die from the heart disease that comes from being inactive and obese. You can hardly be active when you can't even sleep.

Many of us are dying from a heart disease that began a long, long time ago. We were wounded, hurt, abandoned, or forgotten by those that should have cared.

MORE.

So we've learned that instead of being honest with each other and with our God, it's a lot easier just to lie to ourselves and to each other while we smile and say, "I'm doing just great, and you? Oh, praise God." But we're not doing just great. We're dying inside, and the longer we keep quiet, the more certain we are to die.

AND WE WILL, YOU KNOW.

We keep telling each other lies, and we keep being lied to. *You are not fat. You are a child of the King. A child with big royal bones.... You just need to grow into Jesus, and the fat will disappear....*

Maybe, but to me that all sounds a bit queer.

I'm addicted. Pure and simple. My heart is aching; I'm hungry and in need. I may be fat, but I'm a child of God. So tell me: How can I begin to believe? Really believe and then live like I'm free? What power does the God we serve have to offer someone as desperate as me? I've asked Him time and time again for forgiveness and help, but I'm still hungry, addicted, and fat. Now, God, what are You going to do about that?

Are you sick of being fat? Are you tired of religious answers that are even worse than "pat"? There's no more time for that. There's no more time for telling lies, and there's no more time for being fat. It's time to take God at His Word.

JESUS SAID,

"Come unto Me and I will give you rest."...

Freedom from addiction, heart disease, and death.

I once was fat, but now I'm closer to being free. And my heart is not diseased. But first it took honesty. I had to tell the world that the hunger I had for a father led me instead to the arms of a man, where I thought I'd found a place to meet my needs for acceptance, love, safety, and strength. All that and a bag of chips. But the further I went, the emptier I felt…like I had been drinking diet soda instead of drinking milk.

I bet you wish you had skipped this page. But there is a moral to this immoral story. And it will work as well for you as it's working now for me. The God that I serve is a freedom-fighting God who sent His only Son to set all captives free. If we will believe. You take the first step;

tHEn god taKes 33.

Once He begins to free us from being fat, there are some old patterns of behavior we may need to break. Because we all hunger for intimacy and acceptance and love, we need to plan ahead and have the refrigerator stocked with the right things before the hunger hits. If the chicken is already cut, you'll be surprised at how fast you can make something that fills you while it feeds you with the things your body really needs.

We may also need to confess sin on an ongoing basis for a while, as humiliating as that may seem. But our friends will understand because they have the same desperate need. Even if we don't struggle with the same old sin, guess what? This is a very long race, and the longer it is, the more hurdles we have to clear. The harder we run, the more pain we will feel. We need God, we need each other, and we *need* to be free.

But the most important thing we need is a heart transplant, because the old one is just too diseased to be healed. In the Old Testament, there is story after horror story of how the children of Israel became whores by running after false idols. We too have become whores, and whatever our addiction, we're living a real-life horror story. We have embraced idols and junk food and a hideous list of other things that have eclipsed our love for God. That hurts His heart more than it hurts our heart, so instead of using a Band-Aid or angioplasty, the Great Surgeon transplants hearts. We have only to ask. No list, no HMO politics. Just ask.

> "I will give you a new heart and put a new spirit within you;
> I will take the heart of stone out of your flesh and give you a heart of
> flesh. I will put My Spirit within you and cause you to walk in My
> statutes, and you will keep My judgments and do them… I will call
> for the grain and multiply it, and bring no famine upon you."
>
> WWW.EZEKIEL@36.26–29.NET/NKJV

You see? A heart transplant and plenty of food for everyone. There goes our hunger; there goes our need. There goes our junk food, fat, and bondage—and there goes our heart disease. He who the Son sets free is free.

INDEED.

ONE
ONE
TRANSPARENT
SON

THE TRUTH WILL SET THEM FREE WHEN THEY
SEE THROUGH YOU TO HIM IN
REAL TRANSPARENCY

> Then Jesus cried out, "When a man believes in me,
> he does not believe in me only, but in the one who sent me.
> When he looks at me, he sees the one who sent me."
>
> WWW.JOHN@12.44–45.NET

God does things in such remarkable ways. He chose to let go of His position, lose His reputation, and assume the worst possible identity to make His entrance on this earth. For all intents and purposes, He sprang up from the dirt. Although the people around Him must have assumed the worst, He truly was the sinless Son of a godly virgin, and His life was an open Book. The great and invisible God chose to be more visible than most of us ever choose to be. He chose to plant His feet firmly on the ground and allowed the curious masses to see everything He did. He was the quintessential model of pure transparency.

For most of my life, I've tried to be anything but transparent. From a very early age I've tried to hide some things from God, and when I was writing *God.com,* I was hiding them from you. Then, quite unexpectedly, I found myself confronted by the truth and the need for real transparency. There, on the rooftop of my loft in the City of Angels, in an honest gathering of a community of friends that had met to worship and pray, a woman who has an uncanny gift of hearing God speak spoke out, directing her words at me.

"James," she said, "I see you writing your book. I see it being opened and the pages being ripped. And as the pages are being rent, I see you being torn, and I can see right through the pages and right through you into Jesus. Instead of seeing James, readers will see Jesus, and they will never be the same. But first, there must be a real rending and tearing, leading to complete transparency."

About four or five years before that word was delivered on that rooftop in L.A., God had told me that He would not be able to use me fully until I was willing to step out and tell the truth about where I'd been and how I'd sinned. Pain and panic overwhelmed me as I tried to justify my silence while juggling a call from the Most High God upon my life. So when Diane saw that picture of the ripping, rending, and tearing, I knew exactly what that would mean.

When I told Diane the truth of my story and how difficult it was to tell it, she turned a lighter shade of pale. "I don't believe that's necessarily what you have to do," she said. "I don't even know what that picture meant. I just knew I had to tell you."

I knew what it meant, and I was pretty sure there was no way around telling you the truth. But when I went away to write the next chapter, I tried for all I was worth to write anything and everything but the chapter "I Am a Hypocrite." Nothing would come. Nothing would flow except real and painful tears.

NO, GOD. NO. Isn't there any way around this? Can't I write about something else?

His words were warm and gentle, but they were clearer than a bell: *I, the God of the universe, identified with all of humanity's sin. I was sinless and without shame, yet I willingly took on all of mankind's sin. I owned it as my own. Are you, a sinner, unwilling to identify with the sin you did commit? What makes you greater than your Master?*

He was right. (He always is.) Only my own foolish pride could keep me from owning what was mine and what He already had forgiven. Only my fear of being judged by other humans was keeping me from boldly sharing my secrets to a world in so much need. And whether we're willing to admit it or not, this world is in so much need—we are in so much need.

I sit in coffeehouses in cities across America and around the world, and your kids—your junior high and high school kids—think it's fashionable to be "bi." These same kids are fans of shows that celebrate the virtues of being sexually active and undressed, and even before they've reached full maturity, they're majorly oversexed. The things I hear in line at a mall make me wonder what gets talked about in private, if the things that are talked about in public are so open to us all. I'm limited in my imagination, I guess, because I think, *There must be nothing left.*

The world is being a lot more honest than we are. The world is talking about all sorts of dark things that go on in closets and in bedrooms. Isn't it time that we started being more open about the things that God is doing in our hearts and lives to set other captives free?

For some reason, God selected me, someone who was struggling with his identity, to stand before the world and say that I'm a sinner. I'm just one more voice that God has chosen to start a dialogue that will begin to set us free. The most important thing isn't the battle or the sin we must face; what's most important is our decision to continue to believe as we fight, moment by moment, to continue the race.

Let us throw off everything that hinders
and the sin that so easily entangles, and let us run with
perseverance the race marked out for us.

WWW.HEBREWS@12.1.NET

It's too late for us to play games, and it's time for us to quit playing church, because the lives of people all around us are going down in flames. What are we going to do about that? Are we going to hide in the safe little world we've created for ourselves? Or are we going to break down our walls and use the rubble to build a bridge? Are we going to ask to be overpowered by His love and begin to really live like Jesus—that see-through Jew? When we do, those in need will see through us to Him and hear His words of truth, hope, and life and become free of the bonds of sin. Do you realize how much power we have at our very fingertips? Do you realize the power of the words that could be passing through our lips?

There is great power available for every single person willing to believe and then ask. There is great power in the transparency that comes when we step out from behind our mask. I had no idea what the response to my simple confession would be. I simply asked the God of the universe to use it to make a difference for the one lost sheep, even if that lost sheep happened to be me.

So I was amazed to find out just how many one-lost-sheep there could actually be. And in retrospect, I'm so grateful that God cared

enough to have me become transparent—no matter how painfully—
so that at least one other lost sheep would find comfort and the
courage to confess, repent, and begin the process of living free.

> Dear James,
>
> I wanted to write to thank you for being obedient
> and writing this book. You reflected a lot that I have
> suspected or have felt deep down but couldn't express.
>
> Like a lot who have read this, I imagine, I too came
> out of homosexuality and have done the Living Waters
> course and have cried more this year than ever in my life.
> I have also come to a point where moving forward is the
> only option…the other is totally unthinkable, and yet I
> could totally relate to your looking for love that you
> expressed. God dug deep as I read your book, and while I
> am not totally whole, I do know that I am becoming
> my own person…separate from others, with my own set
> of boundaries.
>
> I also agree that the book touches issues that most
> keep taboo in the church, and it angers me that people
> walk under false respectability while so many are dying
> and crying. I say…be blunt, honest, open, and tell the
> truth in love…but don't shut up for anyone. This is some-

thing I'm learning to do. I know that God spoke to me about the false "okayness" that actually alienates others because they feel more alone. Can we in the church not start to address issues of pornography, sexual addiction, and masturbation, etc. that so many discriminate as bigger sins? It drives me livid.

God has really encouraged me, and I am blessed that you were so frank, because I am like that and believe that in this generation, if you are not "in your face" and honest...yet weak and broken so He can be glorified...no one will listen. There are thousands out there who have no hope...it frightens me to think this...may we all move out there and love others...because I realize that when you love others...you get slapped in the face a lot...like God.

Bless You and thank You, Lord, for a book that has encouraged me.

Blaize,
Australia

James 5:16 says, "Confess your sins one to each other." And look what follows: "that you may be healed." Somehow most of us think that our particular sin is the very best kind, so we don't need to confess it, or that it's the very worst kind, so we're afraid to.

That same Scripture says, "Pray for each other." No matter what we need to confess, if we surround ourselves with loving people who are willing to look past what they see and lay hands on us in prayer, we'll find help and acceptance and real community. And when we do, healing will begin.

None of us can do this alone, and honesty is the first step that moves us back toward home. It is possible. I'm making my way there now. And I'm trusting that the God I love, the God I have chosen to embrace, will look past my flaws, my sins, and my shortcomings and see me through this race. I'm going to make it. And you're going to make it too.

God wants us to be transparent so we can go out into this world and begin a revolution in the lives of those we meet. The power that comes from a God who speaks into the lowly lives of those who believe will bring about change that no one can deny, if we are only willing to move past our fear and all that foolish pride. Move past the hiding and into the light of truth and transparency. Confess what you're hiding and allow Him to bring new life through you as you speak the truth about where you've been and where you are as you move more fully into Him.

Dear James,

It seemed so innocent, lying there so quietly on the bookshelf. Maybe that's why I noticed it, because it was so quiet. As I came near, I heard the gentle whisper, "Extreme Intimacy with an Interactive God." I remember thinking, Well, this is what I have been looking for, a closer relationship with Him. But despite the warning label, I expected a light read—maybe
Ten Steps to Getting What You Want from Jesus. Another version of Americanized Christianity; you know, getting to know Jesus better as you become more talented, efficient, prosperous, creative, likable, successful. Becoming more intimate with God as you do your own thing.

I never expected this innocent-looking book to change my life in ways that I do not yet fully comprehend. I did not expect the words in this book to cause me to look painfully into the hidden parts of my soul. And I did not anticipate, as I peered into the abscesses of my heart, that Jesus would whisper words of love and encouragement while I cried over my brokenness.

At first I thought that your idol was different from mine. Now, however, I am not so sure. Maybe only the manifestation is different. The core of my idol is this: I want what I want, when I want it, and I want Jesus to go along with it. Now.

And yes, I have been known to throw stones. You know the type. Sin/idol A is worse than B is worse than C. Thank You, God, that my sin is not as bad as his/hers. Surely materialism, racism, consumerism, and all other "isms" (I want!) are not as bad as—"those other sins"—sexual addiction, drug addiction... But now I can see that my only recourse is to lay my stones down, fall on my face, and cry, "Lord, have mercy on me, for I am a sinner."

An imperfect man living in a rooftop apartment with his imperfect dog—this man having such a love relationship with his Creator that the love of the Creator spills out onto the written pages of a small, quiet book. Who would ever imagine that those words would be so encouraging? Who would anticipate that God would reveal Himself in such a manner?

And this man who wrote this book, what are his credentials? Shouldn't he be a well-known pastor or TV evangelist? I mean, can just anyone have a love relationship like this with the Father? Even someone like me, an imperfect woman living with five imperfect dogs in a house in the desert?

Well...yes! Thank you, James, for this wonderful book.

In Him,
Jessica

Ask God to move mightily through you to mold you into the son or daughter He intends you to be. Don't fear the waiting. Rest in belief while you allow yourself to know as you are known, and allow others to see through you into the Father that they too can call their own.

Just ASK.

Ask, and He will open the eyes of your understanding.

Ask, and He will give you a heart filled with compassion.

Ask, and you will move in the power of His gifts.

Ask, and you'll be surprised at all He gives.

YOU HAVE NOT BECAUSE YOU ACTS NOT

JESUS' FAMOUS LAST WORDS:

"But you will receive power when the Holy Spirit comes on you; and you
will be my witnesses in Jerusalem, and in all Judea and
Samaria, and to the ends of the earth."

WWW.ACTS@1.8.NET

Just before Jesus was taken up in a cloud into heaven, He left
us with some powerful parting words. He made it clear that nothing was to happen, that nothing really could happen, until He left
and sent the Holy Spirit to empower us to bring life and freedom
to those who are enslaved. He said we would receive power that
would work mightily in the lives of those around us, if we were
only willing to allow this Spirit to fill us and flow through us.

Back on that day when His fearful followers waited and
prayed, God showed up in tongues of flame, leaving their tongues
flapping in the God-breathed wind that brought the great change.
You can read the whole account in the second chapter of Acts. No
matter how you interpret what happened in that dynamic display,

the fact is that men and women who had previously lived in a weak-kneed state of half-hearted belief were now filled with a fire and resolve that would transform thousands of lives.

If we look around today, we can pretty much see that we have very little power. We have mega-churches with mega-budgets supporting mega-programs to make the converts comfortable and the seekers safe—all for the benefit of the same old people who gather from week to WEAK.

A.D.D. THEOLOGY

This is not to say that giant churches can't be wildly empowered and effective. God can do anything He wants, any time He wants, and I doubt that He's selective when prayer is the core curriculum and not just an elective.

The manifestation of God's Spirit in the very early church was not seeker sensitive and certainly not politically correct. It was alive, wild, and full of fire. Its message was direct, and its power turned skeptics into converts within just a few hours. The early church moved out and let the power fill them and flow through them to do bold and mighty exploits that grabbed the attention and the hearts of thousands of people at a time. When they would allow the Holy Spirit to fill them, the rest would fall in line, and the church would double and triple in very little time.

It can happen again, if we just ask. Take a walk through the book of Acts. If we look at the church that Jesus intended, we might conclude that some of our polished programs might need to be suspended. Too many slick television shows have gone out on our airwaves, and too few have witnessed the power that comes when we ask for it by name. His name: JESUS.

Programs and organized events aren't nearly as effective as what happens when people are willing to ask to be filled with the power of the Holy Spirit, listen for God's voice, and then obey when they hear it.

Recently I met a group of young men who have chosen to live together in a big old house, praying together, cooking together, and ministering everywhere they go. It may sound freaky or cultlike, but if you read the book of Acts, that's exactly what you'll see: people holding things in common, selling what they have, and living in real and vital community. These five young men pray for hours, allowing the Holy Spirit's power to infect all they do and all they see. They live like they believe while doing what it takes to make ends meet. Their lives come the closest to the early church model of any I've seen.

When I met them, I began to see what happens when we ask for power from on high. They had invited me for dinner and a time of prayer. At the time I was feeling spiritually exhausted, and as I drove to their house, I asked God if He would bless me with more power to move in miracles while I was there.

Shortly after I arrived, Glenn placed his hand on my heart and rubbed some oil on my head. I have to admit that I worried about what the oil would do to my complexion and wondered if it would get into my hair. But within a few short seconds of Glenn's empowered praying, I forgot I even cared, because God spoke so powerfully through him.

Although Glenn knew nothing about my life, his words were right on target. All feelings of doubt and fear left me as I allowed this man to flow powerfully in God's Spirit. My friend Norm happened to be right next to me, and he began to laugh while Glenn was praying. He interrupted the prayer to whisper in my ear, "I haven't told these guys a single thing about you—I swear." But God had, and the results were obvious.

One of the things Glenn asked God for on my behalf was power to move in the miraculous. That was exactly what I had prayed for in the car. God had heard and Glenn had too. For the next several hours a most remarkable display of words and pictures and stories showed me that God was truly there. The power evident in that place lifted me out of my funk, and it didn't take long before I was able to turn the table and begin to pray for my brothers who had gathered to pray for me.

That's the beauty of allowing others to minister to you: You don't have to wait to pour back to those around you; you simply have to allow them to allow the God of the universe to pour right through them into you. Then, with a full cup and with fresh fire, it becomes clear what you should do.

I then asked Glenn if it would be okay for me to take some time to pray for him. He eagerly agreed. He had been giving out so much that he desperately needed to be filled back up. As I laid hands on my new friend, I listened to hear what words God would have me pray, and within a few short minutes I had more words than I could say. They were not my words—they were His—and they were the words that Glenn needed to hear.

Often when people with great gifts minister to us, we shy away from ministering to them because we fear we have nothing as good to give back. But I'm learning that there is a power that transfers—a power exchange that's almost like an apprenticeship. Elijah moved in great and mighty power. He saw fire fall from heaven on more than one occasion because he asked for it by name. Then Elisha became his apprentice, and he asked God for more of the same, a double portion of the anointing Elijah had. And you know what? His request just made God glad. We have not because we ask not, and that includes asking for power from on high. To win the lost in this dark world, we must have the power that God supplies.

Are you tired of being a coward about your faith? Are you tired of just showing up in mega-churches where you have to act all mega-blessed and fake? The truth is that none of us should have to live like that. None of us should be big fat cats in great big churches where the music is great and the preaching ends on time. Church is about the amazing love and power of God, which will put us back on-line with the things that will make the people around us take notice. They can't ignore a God who reads their mail, and if we move in that sort of dimension, they can never out-vote us. They may pass laws forbidding us to speak Jesus' name, but they can never take away the power that will bring life to the dead, vision to the blind, and strength and healing to the lame.

Now is the time for His church to move in power! Are you willing to ask and wait in the upper room, wherever that room may be, to find out if God is good on His Word? Are you willing to begin to do things that at first may feel absurd?

A few weeks after my first visit, I went back to Glenn's house. I took my friend Aaron, who had been floundering for weeks, wrestling with his God. He claimed that he never could hear God speak and that it was eating him alive. He was beginning to wonder if this whole miraculous God-thing might have been contrived. So we went in the hope that this same God would show up in a way that would bring healing and power to my friend's weakened, aching heart.

Again, within a few minutes of walking through the door, I watched as Glenn, that young prophet in training, stood in the living room and, empowered by the Holy Spirit, read Aaron like a book. I wish you could have seen the transformation that played out in that room. My friend who had felt so doomed was now alternately laughing and crying while Glenn spoke words of life. And while I watched, I felt the Holy Spirit prompt me to turn this into a workshop, a place of instant apprenticeship where the same Spirit that was operating in and through Glenn would infuse and work through the heart of my friend. When Glenn had finished his powerful prayer, I asked if we in turn could pray for him.

I began by asking the Father to clear my mind and my heart of all preconceived ideas about the things I thought I should pray and to fill my heart and mind with the words that He would have me say. In a moment, I had pictures in my mind. Often we think these are just distractions, but if we trust and move out in faith and speak about what we see in the theater of our mind, these pictures often show us the very words that God wants us to say. It just takes moving past fear into believe and being willing to make mistakes and look a little foolish while we pray out loud.

In this particular case, I saw some very exotic gifts wrapped in a way that would grace the pages of the world's finest magazines. The lighting and camera angles were exquisite, making it difficult at first for me to see that they were in fact extraordinary gifts.

I spoke these words in faith: "God has given you gifts that are rare and beautiful. They appear from unexpected angles and in unexpected ways…so much so that you and those around you may have trouble identifying them as gifts. But they are astonishing gifts, and God, the Great Director, is lighting them in supernatural ways. As you present these gifts to the world, you will truly be amazed at the results that follow. As you follow."

Although Glenn thought I had been praying those words over someone else, he was privately claiming them for himself, because many people for many years had misunderstood the gifts that God had given him.

I smiled. "They were for you," I said.

Then, in the spirit of the apprenticeship and the passing along of gifts, I asked Aaron to speak out the words that came into his head. I told him that if he saw any sort of picture, not to be afraid to speak out what he thought he might have seen and what it might have meant. My friend was silent for a time. Then he stepped out with a baby step. He prayed and then said that he saw two little girls holding hands. He said that although he could see only two, he knew that in the shadows behind them the line went on and on.

He was a bit timid at first in his delivery, but Glenn interrupted to say how accurate Aaron's words were. Just before we had gathered that evening, Glenn had seen the two little daughters of his good friend holding hands, very much like Aaron had just described, and his heart had been aching because he didn't have children and might never because God kept him single and fully occupied. It seemed that God was using Aaron's picture to remind Glenn that he did in fact have children, more children than he would ever know until he stepped into the land of the promise and looked backwards from the perspective of eternity at the great heritage he helped father by moving in the fatherland of believe.

Hearing this, my buddy, his faith now bolstered by what had just occurred, began to pray with power and authority. His words came out in more thunder and might than I had ever heard. This was a new beginning, and I watched an apprentice rise up that day. I saw God's might and power in the realm of the miraculous wipe the dark clouds of doubt away.

It's no wonder that so many of us who claim to be believers are besieged by all the same things—depression and doubt, exhaustion and addiction—because unless we move in might and power, it's where we all end up. We are weak by nature, and when left alone and unattended, our hearts are desperately wicked. But there's hope: We can move like Elijah did with Elisha. Those of us who have encountered God's power can introduce it to those who have not. We can ask God to pass on the gift to those who want it

and then watch them do even greater works with it because they
are willing and because they believe.

> "'In the last days, God says, I will pour out my Spirit on all people. Your
> sons and daughters will prophesy, your young men will see visions, your
> old men will dream dreams. Even on my servants, both men and women,
> I will pour out my Spirit in those days, and they will prophesy.'"
>
> WWW.ACTS@2.17–18.NET

We have not because we *ask* not and because we *Acts* not.
God's power enters our lives when we are willing to believe and ask
and act. When we ask, He will give, and when we in turn pour out
to others, His power will be magnified as it flows through His
network, and it will allow the desperate and the dying to begin
to really live.

6 POWER
IN THE NETWORK
IT'S THE ONLY THING
THAT WILL MAKE THE netWORK

Very recently, while in the heat of yet another battle (and there will be plenty on the back side of believe), I discovered the net that forms in the company of friends and how I need it to keep me safe so I can discover how the journey ends. There's power in community, that network of trippers God has given us to catch us when we fall— off mountaintops, through clouds of doubt, or anywhere at all.

My friend Paul (of the Paul Colman Trio) told me recently that the fishermen in the ancient Middle East spent nearly 80 percent of their time repairing their nets to ensure a greater catch. But we in the modern Western world do little to repair our nets, so our relationships are suffering, and we're losing many fish.

I COULD HAVE BEEN ONE OF THOSE LOST FISH.

When my battle was raging, it felt like a battle unto death, and I would have died alone if it hadn't been for those of you who were willing to make my burden your own. In your listening and obedience and the e-mails that you sent, you helped this poor warrior break through the cloud of unknowing, doubt, and fear that enveloped me—even as I should have been writing these words. Thank God for His net.

≈ A. D. D. MOMENT ⤸

In this particular battle I had advanced on enemy turf, and the arrows were flying back fast and furious. I wasn't prepared, and if I told you all the details, you would think I'm nuts, if you don't already. Because part of the battle involved my house nearly blowing up. (A case of really bad gas—natural, I might add.) No joke.

Just when I thought I couldn't take one more step, while falling far and fast, I watched the Savior who loved so much spread a huge net out and cast. He cast misfit believers, widows, and paupers—He even used those with so little to offer—but in the casting of the actors and the casting of that net, I saw hope and light again.

God knew that I needed to see and live real community before I wrote another word. The network that Jesus had in mind when He lived out community in the circle of those who were crazy enough to listen, and even crazier to believe, was and is a network that sustains and brings an abundance of life to everyone on this journey to know the Creator of all and the Maker of life. It's all about asking for help, from God and from others who have joined us on this road trip, because this is not a journey we can take all by ourselves. It's a journey we must make in the company of friends.

I'm so thankful for the net that I didn't know existed. I had no idea that this journey could be so hard. That's why so many more are being enlisted—we need each other to help us believe when the battle rages and we nearly grow deceived.

Because we will, you know.

If, like me, you've embarked upon the journey beyond belief, you've probably come dangerously close to giving up and going back to the land where you can see—*see,* that is, in terms of temporal reality. And if you've only just started, you'll soon know what I mean: THE DESERT IS SHUR REAL.

Everyone has a desert—Jesus had a desert, Moses had a desert, and California has a desert. We may not all hear from God all the time, but we will all experience the desert, and in the desert of the real clouds gather quickly after miracles reveal. It's a land where lonely seems more hollow than any vacuum could ever feel.

> O God, You are my God; I shall seek You earnestly;
> my soul thirsts for You, my flesh yearns for You,
> in a dry and weary land where there is no water.
>
> WWW.PSALM@63.1.NET/NASB

(Even David was familiar with the desert of the real.)

Decisions like believe, born of adrenaline and carried on the wings of passion, poetry, and the rhetoric of revolution can take you only so far. This journey is not easy, despite the poetry. It's testing, trials, and sandstorms, and a slew of dancing fleas…so we can grow outside our comfort and live inside believe. Mountaintop experiences are full of glory and great anticipation; from the mountaintops we make our boldest declarations. But the journey beyond those places is filled with desert spaces, and sometimes a long dry spell can make us feel as though our journey beyond belief has led us straight to hell.

HELLOOOOOO….
IS ANYBODY THERE?

There, in those hideous dry places, we begin to realize the depth of our need—a need that makes us run into the arms of the One we truly need and propels us into relationship with one another. This journey will prove Him, it will prove us, and it will prove our friends if we are willing to believe until the end.

If you are troubled by the doubts and questions that keep attacking your decision to believe, know that it was no different for those bumbling few who followed in the footsteps of Jesus. Even His right-hand man denied even knowing Him when things began to hit the fan. Despite their failures and fears, the small **net**work that surrounded Jesus lived beyond the passion and the poetry of sermons served on mounts, last suppers that just didn't end, and even beyond seeing the resurrection of a friend.

The men and women who followed Jesus understood the desert of the real. They knew (and this is a lesson I'm still learning) that the journey beyond belief is not about how we feel.

Because you will feel—a lot.

You'll feel exaltation, exhilaration, and dancing in the streets. So it shouldn't be strange at all if you wake to dancing fleas and sand between your sheets. *And you will, you know.*

I've watched the mightiest warriors be taken captive by despair, but after a few minutes of real, empowered prayer, they were free, back on their feet, and back out in front, shouting war cries of believe.

> "Do not be afraid or discouraged....
> For the battle is not yours, but God's."
>
> WWW.2CHRONICLES@20.15.NET

I NEED GOD.

But I know I need you too, because something powerful happens when two come together on any one thing. The Bible says that one can cause one thousand to run and two, ten thousand. For some reason, God has rigged this thing to make the power that comes from unity operate exponentially. The key to tapping into

God's power is praying with authority, and there is even greater power when we live and pray in real community.

Jesus did mighty things like walking on water, raising the dead, and causing blind eyes to see. Yes, this Savior we call Jesus could make the worst of demons flee. But He said that when we truly do believe, even greater works than His *we* would surely see. Now, maybe I don't live in the right place or know the right people, but I'm not seeing anything even close to Jesus' powerful deeds. So what happened to the greater, and what has happened to believe?

JESUS COMMANDED US TO BE BRIGHT LIGHTS IN A DARK AND DANGEROUS WORLD. HOW DID WE TURN THAT INTO JESUS LITE?

How many times have you sat through carefully crafted eschatological sermons based on the subtle nuances of the lexical meaning of Greek and Hebrew—cross-referenced, overblown, underdeveloped arguments that led to nothing but more arguments? Or, worse yet, sparked absolutely no interest? None.

Y a w n. HUSHED COUGH. Y a w n. CHECK YOUR WATCH AGAIN.

We smiled politely and left, wondering what we had missed on Empty V. At least power is involved when we turn on the TV. The things we've just been subjected to have little to do with you or me or the world in which we make our way. And the preacher seems loath to leave the pulpit because he has so much more to say. Oops—there's no time left to pray.

What has happened to the promise made by the Savior who trekked through deserts and walked upon the sea? What has happened to the power and the miracles? Could there have been some sad mistake in our translation of Jesus' words, or was something lost in the translation—like the power that could put the life back into them? I for one do not believe that Jesus was kidding or a liar. I don't think His words were metaphors. I think this God-man Jesus truly walked on water from dry shore to dry shore. And I think He meant what He said about believe, but He wants us to believe it too. And real revolutions and faith-filled insurrections will rise up when we do.

Not long ago, in that raging battle I've described, I found myself exhausted and near defeat. Dying on the inside, I asked a friend to pray for me. In a kind, Christian way, he did: "Dear Jesus, please comfort James and allow him to feel Your love...."

"Okay, please stop." I said with pain in my voice. "I don't know if you heard me. I'm dying. I don't need to be comforted or feel God's sweet love; I need to be set free so I can truly live."

My poor friend, who meant well, stood up quickly, hoping

that this was all a bad dream.

"What do you mean?" he asked in a small voice.

"I mean that my house is burning down, and you're bringing me an air conditioner. I'm trapped inside a house that's about to burn to the ground, and you're trying to help me by cooling down my living room. I don't want to die in a cool living room. I want to be free."

I realized that I must have had a deranged and desperate look in my eyes. So I explained to my friend, like I'm explaining to you, how to pray with authority to allow the captive to go free. To allow all of us to go free. First, we must confess our own sins to the Father—and maybe even to someone else—so our sin can be forgiven. We cannot enter the Holy of Holies and ask God to do anything at all if we are not clean and whole.

Then, clothed only in His righteousness and covered by His blood, we can stand before the throne. In that place, with the authority of a blood-washed, blood-bought son of the Most High and living God, we can command the worst of the demons to flee.

I know. I've met most of them; trust me.

"In the name of Jesus," my friend started his prayer again, "as a son of the Most High God—" he hesitated a bit and looked at me to see if he was on the right track—"I command this heaviness that is consuming James to leave. Right now, in Jesus' name. God,

I command that Your son, James, be set *free.*"

I think he surprised himself with his boldness. He had been shouting a little too.

But I didn't mind. My house stopped burning, and as my living room cooled, I knew I was free to leave. I could live and love and go set other captives free. But first it had to start with me.

YOU SEE WHAT I MEAN?

The details of this particular battle are relatively unimportant in the entire scheme of things; what's important is what happened when I tapped into the power of the network. The fact is that you need to be surrounded by a company of faith-filled, power-packed friends who can step into the gap when your own will to believe has come to an end. Because there will be days and weeks when it will. And if you have a network of believers around, you will see God step in and work miracles again.

I'm tired of trusting what I know, whom I know, and where I've been—alone. Before, I had only glimpsed the level of my need; but the farther I go on this journey beyond belief, the more I know, and the more I know I need.

I NEED YOU.

This new life has a grand new dimension. It's a life that has more purity, sacrificial love, and grace, so as we meet the needs of others, they will encounter Jesus' face. Not ours. And that's a very good thing. Whatever you do, don't get hung up on yourself. You could forever lose the plot and end up on the shelf.

This is not about you and the things you can or cannot do; this is all about Him and the network that surrounds us—this community of friends. And this is about His power and His willingness to forgive—when we are willing to die and allow Him to live. In us. Through us. With us and for us. The farther you go on the road beyond belief, the less of you there'll be. Less of you, your doubts, and the mountains of unbelief. You'll see more of Him and the things that He alone can see.

No matter who you are, there may come a time when you find yourself in the desert on the back side of *believe,* where you hear nothing from a God who speaks and sand is all you see. Friends can help be your eyes and ears as you navigate that desert, and should there ever be the need, they can help protect you from idols and the false dogs that attract those evil, dancing fleas.

LOVE CAN BE THE PITSTOP

IDOLS AND FALSE DOGS

Journeys through deserts and anywhere in general can be a lot more fun in the company of friends. But it's often difficult to coax someone to go with you through a desert experience—unless, of course, you're married—so we may have to settle for man's best friend. I'd be the first to extol the virtues of big dogs on long hikes. They help you keep up the pace when you tire, and they remind you that you're well liked. (It's so easy to please a dog.)

Today, however, marks the beginning of the end of my journey in the company of my goofy, furry friend. Erich, that most amazing pit bull who walked many a mile with me over the past four years, was ushered out of my life yesterday. Last evening I mopped the last of his paw prints from the kitchen floor, and this morning my bed felt strangely cold.

For the first time in a long time, I'm able to occupy more than a foot and a half of space in my large, insanely comfortable bed. Erich's full-body diagonal stretch left almost no room for me. It didn't start out that way, but because he could move me in my sleep by the sheer force of his body weight and well-aimed head, I usually ended up hanging onto the edge of the bed, while he snored contentedly by my side.

There was something comforting about his rhythmic breathing and even the occasional nightmares that caused him to sob wildly in his sleep. I loved all the wonderful quirks and idiosyncrasies of that big, old, loving dog—all of them, that is, except his prodigal need to run and his remodeling efforts, which involved serious attempts to remove walls, French doors, and chain-link fences. Erich was my foster prodigal son, and the damage he inflicted in his final days with me left me a financial and emotional casualty.

I moved from the rooftop loft in downtown Los Angeles thinking that Erich would be in dog heaven as we exchanged endless plains of concrete under miles of urban sprawl for the majesty of the mountains in an amazing little canyon (only twenty minutes from the city, but a thousand miles away). Erich did in fact love the nature thing. He loved it so much that when he could see it through French doors that weren't open, he worked tirelessly until they were. Usually that involved removing the wood that kept the windows in place.

When I came home from wherever I'd been, my heart would begin to race as I tried to envision what Erich's little mind and massive iron jaws had done. Usually, my vivid imagination couldn't conjure up even one tenth of the devastation. I ended up emotionally drained and afraid to ever leave, and my tree house getaway became more like a prison of fear and trepidation.

A good friend helped me come up with some amazingly clever containment devices. We put up a sadistic little electric fence around the perimeter of the property, strategically placed at pit-bull height. Then I left the remains of the French doors open, knowing full well that with a strange new force in place, Erich would be contained.

He found the whole thing a bit suspicious. His first run-in with the force of the fence was all he needed to realize that some sort of evil surrounded his world. To show me his appreciation, he stayed close to the house, not so much to show his obedience, but to make it easier to take out his frustration by removing the siding of the cabin. It's hard to believe all the damage that resulted from that crazy dog's efforts at deconstruction.

If my landlord reads this, I'll tell him that it was all fiction to bump up sales. But just between you and me, it was more real than I care to believe. I built a kennel out of chain-link fence.

Erich cut a prison-break hole and took a tour of the neighborhood. A kind neighbor invited Erich in, and he promptly killed their cat. I told the manager at Home Depot, and after he realized that I wasn't trying to get a price reduction on my materials, he got a crazed look in his eyes and said, "You have a dog from hell. We've sold a hundred thousand of those kennels, and *no one* has ever had a dog chew through the metal."

Next I used industrial grade chain link. Erich used the higher grade for better grip in order to bend the door right off its frame. Every day began to feel like a race to outwit "dogdini," the most amazing K9 escape artist who ever lived.

I should tell you that I knew that Erich had a reputation when I got him and that I chose to interpret it in the way that best suited me. When I adopted him from the Pit Rescue, I was told that Erich had been turned into the pound so many times that the rescuers had finally deemed his owners "unfit." Who would have ever dreamed that Erich was actually an

Escape-Pit.

For the first three years, Erich was a veritable saint—apart from his fascination with the pigeons at the loft. Everyone who met him raved and gushed and lavishly loved the neck off of him. The only complaints I got were about his tremendously potent gas. Other than that, he was the poster dog for civic virtue. What I didn't realize was that there was just no way Erich could escape either of the lofts I lived in. They were built of metal, concrete, and brick—materials that were impervious to his teeth.

However, when we left the hugely spacious rooftop in L.A. and moved into a place about one-tenth the size, Erich didn't transition well, and I soon realized that wood, glass, door knobs, locks, and gates were no match for this stubborn, bullheaded beast. And I quickly learned that my attempts to create boundaries were not worth the time or energy or *money* I poured into them. In the final days I was beginning to unravel and had no idea what to do. I couldn't trick someone into adopting a dog that had the potential to tear a house down (I tried, but I felt guilty), and putting him to sleep seemed like the only thing left to do.

BUILDING BETTER BOUNDARIES FOR CANINE COMPANIONS AND PRODIGAL, FURLESS FRIENDS.

In dealing with this giant dilemma, it suddenly occurred to me that we often adopt people who are sitting in Pit Rescues. Sure that our love and assistance will help them overcome their demons, we don't realize that it won't take long for their demons to overcome us. A friend mentioned that sin is catching, but that holiness, for the most part, is not.

We rescue these individuals and we love on them. We may even be so generous as to give up our beds. But, in time, if the prodigal desire to run, fueled by out-and-out rebellion, is stuck in their heads, it's sometimes necessary to just let them run, because if we don't, they'll end up running and ruining our lives. No matter how attached we've become or how much fun we may have had, there comes a time to admit that their behavior is just plain bad.

We all have hunger for real and tangible intimacy. Friendships and pets are great ways to get a healthy dose, but it can quickly become a deadly overdose if those friendships and pets take the place that God should get and if they take over your life.

Part of my long, dry desert season involved just such a dog-gone scenario. A very good friend began wrestling with depression and dark unbelief. Although he had witnessed God show up in some miraculous ways, the clouds of doubt and confusion brought on near complete malaise. He began making decisions that brought more darkness, and instead of moving toward the light, he was moving farther away.

I felt it was my place to rescue him, so I single-handedly took on his fight. But the further in I went, the less I trusted God. Somehow I came to think that my friend's salvation was now my job. Even when God began to call me back to that place of intimacy with Him, I ignored His voice because I was so worried about my friend. And that, my friend, is just a kinder, gentler, more deceiving form of idolatry. Because my friend had suddenly become my

main priority, God was going to have to wait while I worked tirelessly to do His job. And He did.

SILENTLY.

It's hard to entrust our friends to the care of an invisible God. But
I'm learning that when I do, He ends up doing a much better job.

I'm not a good one for boundaries. I realize now that my desire
to people please often causes me to give myself freely to people who
end up doing me harm, and I find myself apologizing for things I
have no need to apologize for. The only time I seem to be good at
putting up boundaries is when they keep out good people—people
who could bring healing and love and who could move me toward
my destiny. Those are the people I've been good at keeping at bay.
But for all the dangerous ones, the boundaries seem to melt away.

Thank God for boundaries. I finally read the book by the
same name a few months ago (well, half of it—remember, I have
chronic A.D.D.), and that was all I needed to begin to really see.
We have to take steps to protect ourselves. We can love and we can
give when God indicates that we should. But we have to avoid
giving and loving when it's only obligation speaking, or we may
lose our sanity, our cabins, or our lives.

I miss Erich. He was one of the best dogs I've ever known.
But there was something going on in his great big head—in all

that space that housed his little brain—that made staying home alone in contentment and peace an impossibility. And that made keeping him an impossibility too.

I wonder if there comes a time in a returned prodigal son's life—a time when that raging desire to once again get out of the protective care of his Father and the protection of his Father's house—perhaps on the four-thousand-five-hundredth escape attempt, when the Father finally has to just say, "Go."

If that's the case, I don't believe that the Father loves us any less; in fact, I believe that He loves us all the more. But I know that His heart must hurt more than I will ever understand. Because on the final week before I said good-bye to my big, stinky dog, I witnessed a scene that I will never forget—one that involved a dazed, wet, and shaking pit pet.

In my final weeks of anxiety over what to do with the escape artist who was systematically taking down my house, I visited the vet. He gave me some antidepressants for separation anxiety and a few potent sedatives. I wasn't sure which one of us was supposed to take them. My nerves were frayed, and I was so afraid that my only answer was to put my friend to sleep. But instead, I agreed to try to calm him with the meds.

It was pouring rain that Sunday. I gave Erich a sedative so I could go to church and come home to a sleeping dog instead of to a missing house and missing dog. I came home only to find that Erich, now a feared killer of cats, was wandering the neighborhood in a total stupor, soaking wet and shaking and looking like a heroin addict in search of smack.

I knew it was the end. I grabbed him, carried his soggy ninety pounds up my fifty-five steps, fell on the couch, and held that big, wet, drugged-out dog. I looked at him as he shook, and I finally just broke down. Suddenly, I saw myself in that big, dopey dog. I saw the times that I had tried every imaginable way to escape the net of safety my Father had so lovingly placed around me. I saw the times when I simply rebelled in order to find the things that I thought would thrill, move, or excite me. I saw the times I couldn't stay in, but had to move out recklessly toward more and more sin. Even though, like Erich, I hated to be cold and wet and aimless, it seemed so much more exciting than waiting in the safety of my Father's care…how shameless.

I must have held my dog and cried for nearly an hour. Erich fell asleep while standing, his head resting on my chest. I don't remember ever feeling so much compassion mixed with confusion, but I knew that there was absolutely nothing left that I could do…except let Erich go and do what he thought he had to do.

Life is hard sometimes. The decisions we need to make aren't always crystal clear. But I know that on the other side of my decision to set the boundary that has ushered Erich out, I'm at peace and sane again. I have lost a good old friend. But my life is mine, and the chaos and angst have come to an end.

I'm back to walking this desert alone, and although I'm doing surprisingly well, every now and again I'll trip on a bone—one Erich had hidden somewhere in my life—and I'll miss the great times: the runs on the beach, the games in the streets, and the crazy way that dog could love. But I know it was a season. It's one I'll never forget, but God calls us to new places, and I suspect that some of them don't allow pets.

Don't be afraid to let go. And don't be afraid to love, even though sometimes love can be the pits. But when the journey requires you to create boundaries of protection or to lighten your load, KNOW THAT THE NEXT STRETCH WILL BE BETTER YET.

AN A.D.D. POSTSCRIPT

No pit bulls were harmed in the filming of this scene. Erich was not put to sleep. The fine print on my adoption contract required that, in the event of any trouble, I return him to the Pit Rescue. If you are in need of a demolition job (a whole new twist on *housebroken*), I can give you the number to call.

PART-II

POSTCARDS FROM THE EDGE OF HOPE

A man who has been in another world
does not come back unchanged.

C. S. LEWIS

I learned many of the tips in part 1 on a road trip I took to the bottom (of the planet). It was a journey beyond belief—that trip to the land of the long white cloud with an invisible God. I began the story in *God.com;* here I want to share the details that fell through the net.

This desert journal will take you with me through the back side of believe, where, like a fish out of water, I often found it hard to breathe. I was stripped and tested, battered and bested, but I made it to the end—from the mountain through the desert in the presence of my Friend. I lived on the bottom and I lived on the edge, and now I want to share some postcards from that place, some snapshots of a journey full of truth and hope and grace. His grace. I hope this desert chronicle will bring some comfort in the times that you question as you make your way on your own journey beyond belief.

I've been on a journey to another world, and I've been changed. Here's the rest of the story….

FALLING OFF THE PLANET...
1-900-GOD'SWILL

IF YOU MAKE THE CALL, HE WILL ANSWER.
(But later you may think you dialed a wrong number.)

A long, long time ago in a reality far away, I decided to begin
the journey beyond belief by giving my life away. I had foolishly
told a group of people that after Jesus meets us on the road, He will
ask us to give up our lives to join Him on a trip that will require us
to move out in trust and let go of all that we hold comfortable and
close. After I spoke on this subject, God asked me if I was really
serious. My naive and newfound level of belief was unseasoned and
untried, so I boldly answered God as I looked Him in the eye: *I am
very serious, God. What do You want me to do?*

It wasn't long before the answer came via e-mail. A friend,
Scott, sent me a message from New Zealand telling me about some
people who believed, like I do, that it's possible to communicate the
message of the truth to young people by using television and music
in a unique way. He said that if I hurried and booked a ticket to

New Zealand, he was pretty sure they would be willing to meet with me. I'm usually far more practical than that, but something bigger than me propelled me to purchase a ticket to the land of the long white cloud to discover if this e-mail might have been from God. (You know what I mean.)

When I flew into the tomorrow land of down under, I found that Scott had worked on my behalf and that a meeting had been set. I met a rich lumber baron named Graham, who claimed to believe that the wealth God had given him should be used to reach a generation in serious need. Simon, the guy sitting next to him, was a self-proclaimed genius and the creative director of the program.

They looked a little shocked that I had shown up wearing about a thousand tribal bracelets and earrings and a black T-shirt and jeans. But after some brief and awkward hellos, they handed me their plan. The very first words on the page put me in a state of suspended disbelief. They were the same words a friend had prayed over me back in the States before I left. Seeing those very same words on the business plan of people I had never met made me realize that this road trip was already on God's Palm Pilot and that this was where I was supposed to be. Now I just needed them to invite me to join the team.

BUT THEY JUST WEREN'T READY FOR THE LIKES OF ME.

For three weeks, I waited for their offer with bated breath. But every day that brought me closer to my departure was another day without an offer, and as I neared my very last day, I told Scott about my frustration.

"You don't need an offer from these men, James," he said. "You just need an offer and a calling from your God. The rest will follow."

I thought Scott might have been drinking, but I'd never seen Scott drink. "Okay," I said, my confusion coloring my lie, and made my way to the door.

"James," Scott called after me. "Ask God to do the calling, and then you'll know what to do. You'll be able to walk right up to Graham and tell him that you're coming whether he likes it or not. Then your source will be God, not man."

As crazy as all of this sounds right now, at the time it seemed like a plan. I walked out into the streets of Christchurch and asked God to send me. *Please God, You have to be the One that sends me. I need to know if this is You.* Just then I noticed a window display with some amazingly cool pairs of shoes. I walked inside.

AN A.D.D. MOMENT

Although I'm not a big shopper, I find that distractions,
either attention-deficit induced or just the natural kind
that pop up in shop windows where prices are reduced, are
all part of the way I pray, process, and seek God.
I know; it is a bit odd.

There, a tall, brooding Maori guy greeted me and asked if he could be of help. I said that I was fine. (In retrospect, I realize I had lied.) Then something happened. I looked him in the eye and saw a hurting soul. We started to talk, and he admitted that just the night before, he had wanted to end his life. But first he had yelled up into the black sea that kept the stars afloat, shouting that if God was real, He would have to let him know.

HE DID, YOU KNOW.

Our great God, who I claim speaks, does in fact speak. And sometimes it's through you and me, when we are willing to open our mouths and move into the land I call believe. In the next thirty minutes or so I told this man about a God who loves and a God who cries, a God who wants more than anything to free us from the lies that keep us blind and bound to addictions, devices, and sins—a God who wants to free us if we will only let Him in. I had no speech planned, nor did I think I had anything to lose. I had just come in to look at an unusual collection of shoes.

INSTEAD, I FOUND A VERY DAMAGED SOUL.

When I finished talking, tears were welling up in this man's dark and soulful eyes. While the tears poured down his face, he began to laugh out loud, reminding me of those odd days when the sun breaks bold even while it rains. I saw something powerful enter his heart, and something powerful was about to enter mine. "You know God sent you here, my friend," he said. "He sent you here."

I realized that God was speaking through this man, and even though I had said he couldn't help me, he had helped me more than he could ever understand. I left that store with a new spring in my step, even though I wore the same old shoes, and I walked about an inch and a half above the New Zealand streets as I made my way to the office of my soon-to-be boss with an offer he simply couldn't refuse.

"Hey, mate, I'm coming to join your team," I said. "I've been sent here by God, so I really have nothing to lose." Graham looked pleasantly surprised and then shook my hand with the power and vigor of a New Zealand lumber baron. (And just for a moment I thought he might be admiring my shoes.)

That handshake was the beginning of my journey into the dark land of believe. I was sure that God had called me to go. Now I had to fly back to the States and wait for a call from the guys in New Zealand who wanted me to produce their show.

REVERSE THRUST,
WINGS SHAKE, TESTING THE STRENGTH OF THE WELD.

My scouting trip to the land down under ended when the rubber of the wheels hit the road of the real. It's strange walking back into your life with a secret—one you cannot tell because you don't have proof that it's real. All you know is that you think you know that this secret will forever change your world. But you have nothing tangible—nothing but believe.

E.STRANGEMENT.

At the television network where I worked, I walked the halls with a goofy smile that said *I'm outta here.* I knew I'd soon be flying out that door and heading back through God's own door to the land of the long white cloud and the tall black coffee. The people I worked with thought I'd received an offer of some sort but that I was holding the card until the stakes made it more worthwhile to play. They couldn't have known that I was bluffing. I actually had nothing—nothing but a new confidence that my God had spoken and that I, like Abraham, had to get ready to make the trip to the Promised Land. Still, for a few weeks anyway, I was too stunned, too clueless, and far too faithless to do anything that would indicate I was going to do anything out of the ordinary at all.

As the fumes of my scouting adventure began to fade, things became a bit confusing, and I wondered why God wasn't making it clear what I was to do. In fact I was beginning to wonder if this calling to New Zealand was even really true. Then, in the midst of my confusion, I heard God distinctly speak: *If you are so sure that I've called you to move to New Zealand, why aren't you living like you mean it?*

"I thought that I have been living like I mean it," I responded.

No, if you really believed that you were going to go, you would begin to take the steps necessary to allow yourself to go. Sell your home and your car, and rent your apartment. Take the steps that you can take, so I can do the rest. Then rest.

He was right. I guess that's why we call Him God. I immediately put my house up for sale. It was a three-story, Georgetown-looking thing with three apartments stacked on top of one another. I lived on the first floor and rented out the other two. I realized that in addition to selling the house, I needed to rent out my apartment until the house sold. I asked God to help with that one. Ads in the paper for apartment rentals are pretty expensive, and it can be a real hassle showing to dozens of people and trying to find a person who can pay the rent and won't be likely to burn the place down or paint the walls bright red.

The very next morning I went to my favorite coffeehouse to hang out and read the Sunday *New York Times*. While thinking about what God had told me, I was beginning to get excited about the idea that we can take steps to help further God's plans.

As I sipped my coffee and scanned the headlines, I sensed someone moving toward me. It was a guy in his late twenties. He was standing in line to pay his bill, and he was looking right at me.

"Hey, do you know any apartments in this area for rent?" he asked.

There are some times in life when your jaw really does drop—times when it isn't just a literary expression verging on cliché—and this happened to be one of them.

"I'm sorry.... What did you say?" I feigned momentary deafness because I didn't really know what to say.

"I said: Do you know of any one-bedroom apartments for rent in this area? I'm assuming that you live around here." He smiled and looked as though he suddenly realized how brash and assuming it had been for him to just burst out and ask a stranger if he knew of a place where he could live.

"Yes, I know of a great one. It has a fireplace, hardwood floors, a great private garden, exposed brick, and a really cool galley kitchen. How much are you looking to spend?" I sounded like I was in the business.

"About six hundred or six-fifty." He pulled out a twenty to pay for his breakfast. While he settled up with the cashier, I nervously gathered my things, wondering how in the world I was going to explain this to my friends.

"That is exactly how much this apartment is." I decided the rent just then.

"Great, I would love to take a look. I'm heading back to D.C. today, and I need to see it before I leave. Do you know how I can contact the tenant or the landlord?"

"That would be me," I said. "I'm both."

He looked confused. "Great. Can we head right over then?" I left money on the counter and led this stranger to my car. I lived close by, and within minutes I could tell that the guy was sold.

"I'll have to look at a few more, and then I'll give you a call from D.C. to let you know. How bizarre is this? I ask a stranger about a place to live, and now this."

I was thinking the same thing. God seems to breathe exceptionally hard some days and not at all on others. That day I felt so full of His breath that I thought I might explode, but at the same time I felt nervous and endangered, like I was letting go of something and might have nowhere else to go.

That night as I stood in the middle of my apartment in the middle of my house, I started to wonder just how crazy all of this

was. Could that guy have been sent from God to help me understand that something big was at work here, even though it seemed
that nothing was at work at all? And even though I had this new
burst of faith, I felt it start to fall when I thought, *What am I
going to do with all my stuff? I can't rent this place out while I have
all this stuff!"*

POSSESSIONS OR POSSESSED?

I checked my voice mail. "Hey, James, this is Sam. I will take
your place. Give me a call, and I'll give you my address so you can
send the contracts."

Suddenly, with an interested party talking about contracts and
the thought of losing my home, I was too overwhelmed to call him
back. I thought it wouldn't kill him if I waited a day. Besides, I had
to figure out what I'd do with all my stuff, and I really didn't know
what to say. So I didn't.

The next morning the phone served as my alarm. It was Sam.

"Hey, you never called me back. Can I rent your place, or not?
I'll need to move by August. Oh, and I was also wondering if you'd
sell me all your things. I really don't have much, and I like what you
did with the place. So if you want, I'll buy them from you."

I put down the phone. It seemed that I was heading out of
town and that I wouldn't have all that much to pack. It also started
to feel like there was to be no turning back.

I GUESS I TOOK THE RED PILL, NOT THE BLUE.

As you can see from the mundane details of my first big journey beyond belief, minutiae play a part in making a decision that will forever change your life. Mostly, though, it involves the ongoing decision to believe past what you can see. It involves a willingness to know that even when things don't turn out like you plan, still all of it is tucked safely in God's hand. Somewhere in the hollow of His hand.

SKY, SEA, OR LAND.

If I take the wings of the morning or dwell

in the uttermost parts of the sea,

Even there shall Your hand lead me,

and Your right hand shall hold me.

WWW.PSALM@139.9–10.NET/AMP

THE PROMISE(D) LAND(ING)

PROMISES, PROMISES.

We often make them, can rarely keep them, and are devastated when others break them. Promises are difficult, especially for me. I expect all the people in my life to keep their word, but I can't keep mine. That's the irony.

I'll promise you a dream—something much bigger than you or me, something you've always dreamed about, even though you can't quite remember what it was.

AUDIO FADE.

SOUND EFFECTS:

DRUMS BEATING;

CHILDREN LAUGHING

OVER MELODIC TRIBAL CHANT.

I'll promise it in great color and texture while playing a jingle—a world-music-epic one that makes you feel you're a part of a very special club.

VIDEO INSERT:

SLOW-MOTION MONTAGE OF CHILDREN FROM **EVERY** TRIBE AND NATION, SMILING, LAUGHING, AND DANCING WITH THE AGED.

You look into my eyes (and they are honest eyes) and buy in hook, line, and sinker. The sad part of this honest tale is that I'm not always able to make the reality play out with the same intensity of the dream. The sound track loses time, subtle details get lost in the film transfer, and particulars get dropped.

I'd like to blame these broken promises on A.D.D., but my disorder didn't do it; it's part of my history. I think that when I was swimming around in that womb without a view, I was under the impression that I was going to be welcomed into the loving arms of a mother and a father who would fight until the end of time to help make this journey called life just a bit better than sublime. I think I even saw that cute couple signing on some sort of dotted line. But that promise didn't last, and I ended up a product of a broken home before I was even housebroken. And that was the beginning of a journey on which a fragile heart was broken again and again.

I'm not at all vying for your sympathy or trying to win your undying love and support. I realize that my story isn't rare, and I'm not a spoilsport. Mine is just one of many stories that make up the anthology of the broken in this hurting world in which we live. I'm just trying to make an important point:

WITHOUT TRUST
IT IS ALMOST IMPOSSIBLE TO
EMBRACE TRUTH

I think that living in a land littered with empty words and shattered dreams tends to make us distrust the Maker of eternal promises and the God of all our dreams.

I know I do.

Even as I made my way on this journey called believe, I was always ready for the other shoe to drop—for the day when I'd read in the headlines that God was in fact dead and that I had fallen for some sort of cruel cosmic joke that had robbed me of my credibility. Then it would be too late to go back to the land of skeptics, atheists, and Democrats. I would forever be banished to one of those scary refugee camps where I would have to wear an ugly, gray-striped jumpsuit and a telling yellow star, and I'd have to drive around in a controlled suburban ghetto with a plastic fish stuck on my car.

A HIDEOUS A.D.D. MOMENT

You know, we are already being marginalized,
like Hitler marginalized the Jews. He used a propaganda
machine to begin to turn the screws. Our media today
remind viewers around the world just how foolish those
who believe can be. We smile and pay for tickets
while we're slandered mercilessly.
Welcome to the last bashable minority.

Or I wondered when God would finally really look at me and all I'd done and all I'd been and tell me and everyone else that the jig was finally up and that this sham artist was really not a good guy and really not a friend. In fact, I imagined that He might even say that I was an **enemy of the state** of affairs in the places where I desperately tried to fit in.

But God already knew everything about me and everywhere I'd been. He saw my broken heart and the broken promises that helped break it, and He continued to pour out His love, grace, compassion, and favor—while doing everything inhumanly possible to help my heart mend.

HE STILL IS.

But back in the days when I was trying to figure out what God was doing and what He was trying to say about the trip to New

Zealand, there was no end to my confusion as I clung to a promise I thought had come from an invisible God. In fact, the days when He seemed absent felt like full-blown fiascos while I waited to see what I was to do to make His wild promises finally come true.

NO CLUE.

That's the beauty, really. Often we don't have, and maybe shouldn't have, a clue. We should be left in the dark while we wait for God to do what only He can do. He's the One who fulfills the promise, not us. Because—and how simple is this?—we didn't make the promise. He did. Therefore it must be His job to fulfill the promise and make our journey begin.

That was pretty much the case with Abram and Sarai. These two greats of the faith had been given some pretty incredible promises by an awfully amazing God. God promised Abram that he would be the father of His chosen people, the nation of Israel. The funny thing was that Abram was pushing one hundred, and that had nothing to do with the speed limit. He was old. His body was not capable of doing what bodies need to do to father one child, much less an entire nation.

4063 B.V. (BEFORE VIAGRA®)

Sarai was no freshman of the faith either, and she laughed in the face of God when He made a promise that seemed so odd. I don't think God minds it when we laugh. I think He's concerned only when we choose not to believe. And in the end, God had the last laugh when Sarai did conceive.

AND SHE DID, YOU KNOW.

I'm learning what a real gentleman God can be: He shows just how much He cares for those who are willing to believe. He took great care to comfort Abram by giving him a glimpse of the light at the end of a tunnel. God Himself took Abram outside to direct his attention to that limitless black sea where stars float in galaxies… and He made a powerful promise:

> "Look up at the heavens and count the stars—
> if indeed you can count them."
> Then he said to him, "So shall your offspring be."

I think the look at the heavens was a symbolic gesture. God wanted to take Abram's eyes off the things of the earth—the darkness that surrounded his current circumstances and his own sagging sense of worth—so He caused him to look up. There, in the night sky, Abram saw God's limitless imagination and power displayed in a grand array. And there in that limitless sea of possibility, he found it possible to say, "I believe."

In that very tangible encounter, Abram reached deep inside an old man's well and pulled up a bucket of believe. And that little, leaky bucket seemed to be all a dry old man would need. God would do the rest, and Abraham could rest.

ONLY THE NAMES WERE CHANGED TO PROTECT THE IMPOTENT.

It helps to have a bright spot to look at when you are holding on to a promise growing dim. Our most thoughtful God gave Abraham three hundred zillion bright spots when He directed his attention to the sky to get a glimpse of what He had in mind when He made a promise to supply. Our God does supply. It just seems to take Him so long sometimes.

That's how I felt after I rented out my apartment and would soon be living on the floor of a generous friend. It felt like this crazy waiting game with God was never *ever* going to end.

IN TOTAL DEPENDENCE DAY.

Finally, I lost my patience with God's timetable. On the morning of July 4, I had a full-blown fireworks display. I had reached the end of my rope, and I blew up at God in a most embarrassing way. I remember filing some specific complaints. I had been obedient and done everything I knew how to honor His request and prepare as if I really would be leaving in August. Now it was July, and I soon would be homeless. With no job offer from New Zealand, I was quickly losing ground. Making it clear that I was on my way out, I had turned a great promotion down. What on earth could God be thinking? I literally shouted in anger until my words became a cry. I felt so confused by this silence, both from God and man—specifically the man in New Zealand who had seemed to have a plan.

Now I was feeling that I had somehow been duped, and I gave God an ultimatum. Because He is kind and forgiving, I imagine He must have been smiling a bit to cover the pain and embarrassment of seeing a son struggle so hard to get his way when he knows it is always His way when we turn over the reins. I told God that if I didn't hear something from New Zealand by the end of the day, I was going to go out looking for a new place to live and find out if I could jockey that promotion despite the smug way I'd turned it down.

I lived in a quiet kind of anxiety for the remainder of the day. Even before the fireworks began that evening, I had completely forgotten the ultimatum I had given God. I think my head was simply swimming, treading water to survive while the white caps of impatience buffeted me in my ocean of confusion.

Explosions and bold bursts of color redirected my attention to the heavens, and I was quickly lost in the pyrotechnics that filled the evening sky. Somewhere before the finale, I lost my anger and confusion, and when the fireworks were over, I made my way home and crawled into a cold and lonely bed. Just as the down of the pillow began to engulf my head, the phone rang. Who in the world could be calling at this hour? Most of my friends knew I was a morning person and didn't appreciate getting late-night calls.

"Hey, mate, Graham here. I don't know why I'm calling you right now, as I'm in a place that is not at all private or convenient and I'm terribly late for my next meeting. But I just felt that I needed to let you know that we are extending a job offer and that we want you to come to New Zealand as soon as you can. I will call back tomorrow to give you more of the plan."

Remembering my ultimatum, I nearly dropped the phone when I looked at my watch. God had waited until the eleventh hour to let me know His plan. So at two minutes before midnight, knowing that He was weaving a grand adventure, I crawled back into a much more comfortable bed, thinking, *God is as good as His word, and He most certainly is not dead.*

I BELIEVE THE ROAD TRIP IS FINALLY ABOUT TO BEGIN.

FOOL'S GOLD, GOD'S FOOL 3

THAT'S ONE L OF A DIFFERENCE

THE ALCHEMY OF BELIEVE.

It all feels like a hazy dream now. I see it in slow motion with a slight drop frame and a bit of that oversaturated color characteristic of the Kennedys' home movies at Kennebunkport. John John waves slowly at the camera while Caroline runs on the beach with herky-jerky, camera-stuttered steps, chasing a big old friendly dog, both child and beast chasing after waves.

As time ebbs and flows, it seems that we all keep chasing after waves.

And I remember those final waves—the waves of mixed emotion and the waves of great old friends—as I pushed off from the eastern shores of these grand United States. I remember the conversations, the smells, the final party, and the final parting. I also remember a good friend, a true seeker, handing me a book by Paulo Coelho, *The Alchemist.*

In the story, a boy leaves his family and friends in Spain for Tangiers and the Egyptian deserts in pursuit of a treasure and his destiny. Upon landing on foreign shores, he is given a cup of hot tea just before he is robbed. The robbery and other hardships almost cost him "believe," but he pushes on, and after passing through harsh deserts, storms, and trials, he discovers the fabled magic of a practice called alchemy.

GO D GOLD.
ALL THAT GLITTERS ISN'T GOD.

ANOTHER L OF A DIFFERENCE.

Some would call it a new-age fable, but to me, new- or old-age, it was an amazingly accurate picture of my journey to New Zealand in search of my destiny. The days leading up to my departure had been just like the book said:

WHEN YOU PURSUE YOUR DESTINY, THE ENTIRE UNIVERSE CONSPIRES TO HELP YOU.

It seemed as if the entire universe had conspired to help me rent my apartment, get rid of all my stuff, and even hear from the guys down under just after I'd told God that I'd had enough. God is the Creator of the universe, and He can use any portion or every portion of it to help us move with speed and accuracy to a place where we can fulfill our calling. Our purpose. Our destiny.

And then there was that CUP OF TEA AND A ROBBERY.

When I stepped off the aircraft and onto that foreign shore, the craziest thing happened. As I descended the stairs to customs in the Auckland airport, a strange woman offered me a "nice cup of tea." She worked for the government, but it still seemed awfully strange to me. I smiled at the similarity of the boy who had landed on a foreign shore before me in that little book about destiny. As I sipped the sweet tea, I was completely oblivious to how bitter the taste soon would be.

After retrieving my luggage (a lot of it, I might add), I began pulling and pushing the "trollies" stacked with my huge boxes.

"I really should learn to pack a bit lighter for these weekend getaways," I joked with the fellow travelers around me. I thought I was being friendly.

But the customs officials who overheard must have considered my jokes suspicious remarks from a cocky American tourist. Within minutes I was standing face-to-face with two agitated agents who asked me several stern questions about my reasons for being in New Zealand. And before I knew what hit me, I heard their stamp hit my passport:

THREE DAYS.

I had been robbed of the three-month visa routinely given to every tourist visiting New Zealand. The sickest feeling you can imagine followed that frenzied encounter with customs. I couldn't figure out how I could go within seconds from a welcome tea to a robbery—both served by government employees. And that was only the beginning. Even though I was able to work out the customs issues within the allotted three days, that skirmish marked the beginning of battle in a desert that left me forever changed.

I had been hired to create a television program that would be groundbreaking and life changing—something that would introduce a lost and hurting world to a message of hope and the Giver of life. But as in any cosmic mission, there was no end of hardships, struggles, hurdles, and delay. In fact, the creative director created such roadblocks that it looked as if our production would never get under way.

In a very real sense, there was a great need for some divine ALCHEMY... because to create an internationally recognized program (which was the goal), we would need a miracle. Television programs are generally produced in large urban centers and have huge budgets, wildly creative teams of people, and resources to spare. So doing a project in a tiny edit bay on the South Island of New Zealand with a team of four or five seemed absolutely ludicrous. Kiwis are proud of the fact that they can surprise the world by making almost anything out of nothing, but since I wasn't an authentic Kiwi, I needed God to provide those results. (Besides, you can't use number eight fencing wire to edit TV shows.)

Finally, after months of resistance and inaction on the part of the creative director, my boss finally gave an ultimatum. "I'm leaving for Hong Kong in eleven days to present a show to the world at a giant television expo. Your job"— he looked at both of us expectantly—"is to create and complete a show by that time." I felt my stomach sink in fear. And with good reason, for one day later the creative director disappeared. The only explanation his wife offered was: "Simon isn't here." She thought he might have gone off fishing in the glaciers.

Graham was livid. He looked at me with a very red poker face. "Well, do you think you can do this on your own, mate?" I smiled weakly and said that I guessed I could. I don't believe I spoke with enough conviction for a wealthy lumber baron from New Zealand, who was less familiar with television than he was with Kiwi wood.

I jumped in my old beat-up Landcruiser and drove wildly up the winding roads of the lava flows to my favorite quiet God-spot…to find out what GOD KNOWS.

I parked the old beast on **Godley Head** and began to climb the cliffs, following the worn-out paths of sheep. I climbed and climbed, trying to work off the frustration born of fear. I tried to hold in all my anger and fight back stupid tears. "God, where in the world are You?" I shouted from a sheer rock cliff overlooking a crystalline New Zealand sea. "God almighty, where are You? Don't You have anything to say to me?"

I must have screamed at God for about three hours. I had risked my world, my reputation, and everything I believed to move to a land of promise, only to find myself deceived. Absolutely nothing had been done on the program in the months and months I had been there. The creative director had been hiding behind a facade of creative mystery to keep our boss at bay.

When my throat was raw from screaming at God, and He kindly wasn't responding in kind, I decided to sit in silence, in case He needed some time. In time, God spoke. He suggested that I sit and watch as He painted the evening sky. I watched as nightfall descended and the stars filled that vast sea above the ocean. I watched until God's work was done. *I go before you and I stand with you. I will not forsake you; you are My son.* I recognized the reassuring tone of the voice of my God. *Rest, and know that I will make a way where there is no way. I will create rivers in the desert, just as I created that glorious sun.*

God continued to tell me of His great plans and how He planned to give me the land as far as I could see, but my only concern at the moment was with making thirty minutes of groundbreaking TV. *Be still and know that I am God. Be still and know that I will provide. Be strong and courageous and know that the battle is not yours—it's Mine.*

I climbed down cautiously from those precarious cliffs, following the well-worn paths of sheep. Then I climbed quietly into my Landcruiser and drove home where I would sleep.

WRAPPED IN GOD'S OWN PEACE.

The next morning, as I was reading through His Word, I found peace despite the dwindling days. I had nothing in mind and hadn't even booked an edit bay, but just as I was finishing my time alone with God (this time there was absolutely no yelling), my head exploded with bold ideas, and I ran to the table and wrote feverishly until the entire show poured out and paper covered the floor.

God gave me a model—a whole new way to do TV. He showed me that the most important part was not spending loads of money or hiring a giant crew. He showed me the things I already had and what I was supposed to do. The entire program came together in ten days. Everyone in our circle was genuinely amazed. And although human nature demands all the credit (I was listed as director), God alone deserved the praise.

In the land down under, I learned that God is the greatest and only true alchemist. He takes common things and, through the intensive heat of the desert, works miracles that transform common people like you and me into His finest gold. But first we must be willing beyond belief to fight through fires of testing, sandstorms in the burning desert, and a circus of dancing fleas.

The alchemists spent years in their laboratories observing the fire that purified the metals. They spent so much time close to the fire that gradually they gave up the vanities of the world. They discovered that the purification of the metals had led to a purification of themselves.

The Alchemist, 84–5

I also learned that carrying crosses is not a romantic pursuit. Despite comforting words of promise spoken by prophets, I still had to live in the truth.

LIFE CAN BE HARD and road trips are trying until the end. We may never get quite what we expect, but we will always gets what God intends.

FareWELL MAY BE welFaRE IN REverse

What if you risk it all by walking away from comfort and safety and a great bunch of loving friends, only to find that you are homeless, vanquished, and destitute in the end? When you choose to take this road trip—this journey beyond belief—is there any traveler's insurance or a money-back guarantee?

WHAT ARE WE TO BELIEVE— THE PROSPERITY MESSAGE, OR "TAKE UP YOUR CROSS AND FOLLOW ME"?

Keep in mind that the cross was an instrument of execution, not a fancy term for a golf bag. Jesus carried a cross, but at the end of His journey, He didn't play a great round of golf; He experienced an extremely severe loss—His life. If we look at Jesus' journey as a model for our own, why are we surprised when our steps falter under the weight of the cross He has chosen for us to bear? Why are we so alarmed and so unsettled when we suddenly find ourselves alone and drowning in despair?

All you need to do is examine Jesus' brief life here on earth to see that hardship, darkness, and deserts are all part of a plan. We are being tempted, tried, and tested to learn all we possibly can. I would prefer a much simpler course, with a generous handicap and no one watching me keep track of my score. But the God of the universe is teaching us so much more—something eternal:

> "If anyone would come after me, he must deny himself and take up his cross daily and follow me. For whoever wants to save his life will lose it, but whoever loses his life for me will save it."

WWW.LUKE@9.23–24.NET

I think we've come to believe that prosperity and success are the natural results of following an invisible God. Lay it all down and watch Him give it all back. And then some. Many Bible stories even support that sort of thinking. God allowed Satan to wipe out Job on a whim, but in the end, Job got back far more than he had lost. Abraham picked up and left behind everything he knew to follow the promise of an invisible God, and he scored as the father of a nation. But despite all the messages that tout prosperity, there are many examples, too many to recount, that are much more in line with Jesus' command to "take up your cross and follow." And the story after that is a little hard to swallow.

I CAN RELATE.

After a year of hardship and angst in the land of the long white cloud, I found myself baffled by the way the details then played out.

The program I created was rushed off to Hong Kong, where someone recognized its virtues and began to praise its worth. The next thing we knew, it was nominated for an international award—The Golden Rose of Montreux. I'd never heard of it, but I was told that it was the world's most prestigious award for light entertainment television. (Until then, I thought that would be an Emmy!)

As our hopes for the Golden Rose rose, our humility shrank in size. We began to have ridiculous little arguments about titles and credits and all the other vain things our world deems so important. We quickly forgot our program's message—love and peace and unity—and began to ask, "Who gets to keep the gold?" and "What's in it for me?" We even quarreled about silly things like if the national press were to pick this up, who would get to speak? In His infinite mercy and grace, God allowed us to continue in our childish ways, knowing full well that He was about to teach us a few lessons.

In the middle of all the preparation for this international nomination, I heard God speak clearly to me about something that was going to happen. He said that I would win a Golden Rose for Best Human Values. This was a very specific award, and only one would be given.

Since the message of our program was all about hope and life and caring, it seemed to make sense that we would win this award, so I shared God's message with my boss. After giving the matter some thought, Graham decided that we should attend the awards ceremony in Switzerland. The Kiwi dollar was at a low, so for him to pull the cash together meant that he believed I'd heard from God. Graham spent a lot of his own money to make it all happen, so now I was hoping that the promise I'd heard wouldn't be broken.

Sure that we were coming home with a Golden Rose, we packed our bags and headed off to Switzerland. When we arrived in Montreux, we were immediately immersed in a round of parties where we mingled with other producers and directors from all over the world. We hoped that winning this award would buy us time and interest from others outside our immediate circle. Meanwhile, we were nearing the bottom of our cash reserves, and Graham continued to remind me how important winning the award would be.

The night of the gala awards finally arrived. We were dressed in black-tie and our spirits were high, but somewhere on the journey between the hotel and the Grand Palais, Graham made it clear that he intended to keep the Golden Rose—the one we hadn't quite won. I don't think I've ever felt such a mixture of elated and undone. Although our program was all about goodness and light, I don't think I'd ever felt more hateful or so full of spite. I was childish and sullen and feeling that I had been severely burned. I mean, I had created the program—shouldn't I take home the golden trophy?

"What went wrong when the other alchemists tried to make gold and were unable to do so?" "They were looking only for gold," His companion answered. "They were seeking the treasure of their destiny, without wanting actually to live out the destiny."

The Alchemist, 132

I don't know why I'm relating all these embarrassing secrets. God has had to be wincing most of the time that I've been living. Because of my horrifying attitude that particular night, He would have to do some serious forgiving.

This journey beyond belief is merely a road trip. If you've ever gone on one with someone you thought you knew, you were undoubtedly surprised to find that person was actually an evil, selfish troll disguised as a very close friend. (And they think the same about you!) That's because when we move outside our comfort zones, we lose the pads protecting our Kmart-thin veneer of manners and polished Christian grace and expose much more of our flesh.

But that's also the beauty of road trips and this journey. If we don't see what's down deep inside, we'll never think we have to change or be changed, and we'll reek with foolish pride. I'm grateful for the blooming bruises that we gather along the way, because without those flowering, purple blemishes, we would always stay the same.

ALL THAT GLITTERS IS NOT A ROSE.

We flew home without a rose, but we had earned the thorns we carried back in our flesh. Although no one said anything out loud, I knew my credibility as one who hears from God had taken a lethal hit. I could hear the subtleties of pain and scorn in Graham's tone of voice. It was suddenly becoming clear to me that leaving New Zealand would be my only choice.

A year of my life, all my savings, and everything I had come to believe about a great God who speaks now felt like so much chaff, and I hadn't even seen the wheat. This was the biggest blow my trust in God had ever received. That infinite and amazing God suddenly lost His luster, and there was nothing that resembled love, faith, mercy, or kindness in the question-mark-shaped void in my severely damaged heart. What kind of God would leave His trusting son so high and dry? What kind of loving God would see this kind of pain and just stand idly by?

I had no reputation. I had nothing to fall back on, and my faith was on vacation. This was a crisis of the soul, and when you're in that sort of crisis, it's difficult to know just what to do or how to do it. So in a very short time I made up my mind to head back to the States to sort out my life in light of the foolish decisions I'd made.

...THERE'S NO PLACE LIKE HOME, THERE'S NO PLACE...

(props: red hiking boots; sound effects: heels clicking together in hope and desperation)

I could only hope that back home some sort of miracle would pull me out of this very real abyss. Even though I now speak of the net of God's great care, it seemed to me then, all those years ago, that God's net was just not there. I felt burned out, bummed out, and completely in the dark as to what God could be thinking. Or was He even thinking at all about my failed journey beyond belief? I didn't have a job and I didn't have a home, which made it even more difficult than it had been to quit one and sell it all in pursuit of a dream. It felt like a nightmare: My life was coming apart at the seams, and I didn't know when or how or if I was going to wake.

On top of the financial chaos and the aimlessness that comes from not having a job or place to live, my mother, a God-fearing woman, decided that I must have

FLIPPED my lid. (That's a line that

was popular in the sixties, I think.) "You told me you heard from God," she said, "and you've come back with nothing to show for it. Nothing at all. That is not the God I serve." Those were just a few of the welcoming words that made up my ticker-tape

HOMECOMING TIRADE.
(Mom, don't be mad. I've said worse things in haste, and I don't have time to list all your good traits.)

But Jesus' words hit me harder than the words of my family just then. He said that unless we are willing to forsake our father and mother, we are not worthy to be His servant, much less His friend. I think I was beginning to understand the confusing verse that says we cannot be pressured by family loyalty or our innate need to please if we are going to continue on with Him on this treacherous road trip of believe. The details from that time are all a bit hazy, but I remember clearly how much it hurts when your family thinks you're crazy.

I couldn't make sense of the yawning abyss I had somehow fallen into, and it felt as though I couldn't fall much farther before I hit bottom. A sickening sort of miasma engulfed my waking moments. Nightmares filled my sleep. I was pretty certain I was on the fast track to destitution—and it had all started with "believe."

At every turn I was reminded of the stupid decision I had made to let go of the safety of my old life and trust a God who now seemed to be a flirty, flighty, capricious little sprite. It was like a perilous dance with near financial and emotional ruin in an oasisless desert of unanswered questions.

On top of everything else, the home I owned had never sold. All three apartments were rented, but the house was desperately in need of some costly repairs. I remember walking into the apartment that had once been mine. The bathroom ceiling had collapsed into the tub. A horrific crop of mushrooms had been thriving up above. I had no idea how I could repair that, much less cure all the other household ailments afflicting that aging abode.

Sitting on the damp hardwood floors that had recently begun to bow, I couldn't even think straight as the need around me just seemed to grow. I had nothing in my reserves—only the possible cash from the sale of the crop of mushrooms that was flourishing in the ruins of my ceiling, now planted in the tub. It seemed that every last trace of the great Creator had been erased, His voice lost in the sound of the madness of my efforts to survive.

❧ AN A.D.D. MOMENT
(THE PAUSE THAT DIGRESSES)

If you haven't had second thoughts yet about taking this road trip with an invisible God, I bet you do now. But I need to be nakedly honest with you about how treacherous the road can be as we continue on our journey toward our destiny. (Do you like mushrooms on your pizza?)

Suddenly, at that very moment, I remembered Richard Wurmbrand, a man of faith who wrote several bestselling books about his years in communist captivity. There he learned a secret that now made this captive free. In one of his mud-lined prisons, he began to worship the God of the universe in the midst of his own personal hell. He began to sing and shout and praise, and in the middle of the bleakest moments, he felt his faith revive. Joy replaced despair, and in a few short minutes of lifting Jesus' name above his circumstances, his darkness was dispelled.

I remembered that man and his remarkable story. And maybe

because I had run out of all other options, I decided to thank God for the things I actually had. It was difficult at first, and I think God must have picked up on the cynicism that mixed with my prayer:

Thank You, God, that I have ceilings that can come crashing down. I know there are a lot of people who don't even have a roof over their heads—or at their feet, as is the case in this bathroom. And thank You for hardwood floors that can warp. I'm thankful that I have walls that can crumble, and I'm grateful that You are teaching me to be humble, because I'm not in a position to be anything else.

Although my life was a mess, I at least had life, and, among other things, I did have breath. The more I gave thanks and the louder I prayed, the more my attitude began to inexplicably change. As my demonstrative praise drowned out my anxiety, anger, and unbelief, I started to experience real, supernatural relief.

MY CIRCUMSTANCES, HOWEVER, REMAINED THE SAME.

It had to be supernatural because nothing had changed in the natural. The house was still a complete mess, but suddenly my heart had been remodeled. I had experienced some sort of spiritual breakthrough. (It's something that's been tested in Romanian prisons and mushroom-farm apartments, so it just may work for you.)

I left the house with a new sense of hope and a very tangible peace. I shared this story with my former boss's secretary, and she celebrated my spiritual victory with me. After she had reflected on my situation for a moment, she asked, "Have you checked with your insurance on covering any of these damages?"

BLESSED INSURANCE.

I took Dottie's advice and made the call, and within a few short days there was more money than I needed to make all the repairs, all because of a decision to look beyond the moment and live in a place of thanks, trading my prison of defeat for a new land of praise.

I continued to live in that place of freedom secured by ongoing praise. Despite my homeless and unemployed state, I sensed that God derived pleasure when I looked past my circumstances and believed that He could easily handle the rest—when I chose to live beyond confusion, anxiety, and unbelief and moved deeper into trust.

Life went on. God provided a new job for me on the other Coast, and that led to my new life in L.A. If you've read *God.com,* you know that that leg of the journey had its own set of challenges, but the main lesson I learned was that God is there no matter what anyone might say. There's hope on the other side of death and on the other side of the grave, so praise past what you can see and give thanks for what you have instead of grumbling about what you need.

LET GO & SERVE

GETTING WITH THE PROGRAM (GOD'S)

Life in the desert is never easy. But I've come to believe that desert times are more instrumental in crafting our character and shaping our resolve than any other time or place in our lives. Mountaintops are great—the views can bring tears to your eyes—but profound, life-changing lessons seem to come in desert storms, in those crazy locust swarms, and in the battle to live victoriously on this journey beyond belief.

I don't know about you, but I've always wanted to be famous. I've crafted how my life should look and what the press would say and how my fans would love me. I thought I would somehow be God-famous—one of those heroes of the faith who gets invited to speak at 50 million giant events and spectacles, someone who's on the A-list and always in demand. (Funny, though, that doesn't seem to be God's plan.)

I always felt that part of my fame would be a result of the profound television I try desperately to make—the kind that doesn't sell a lot of commercials because the content isn't fake.

Well, funding for all programs comes from selling commercial breaks, and when you move outside that reality, it takes divine intervention to make your program sell at all.

Not too long ago, a new network set out to create a whole new way to communicate who God is to people who have seen and heard everything. They were hoping that this audience was in search of some honest answers to life's biggest questions, if they were asking them at all. Once again I thought (subconsciously, I might add) that this might be my chance to become famous as I fulfilled the great commission of God and the network heads. My role in the project was to create a new format and then produce, direct, and assemble a finished show.

It wasn't long before I had a million great ideas running around my head. But somewhere along the way, I stopped and prayed a prayer that I never could have known would cause so much chaos and insecurity—and yet also teach me one of the greatest lessons I may learn in my entire life:

> Whoever exalts himself will be humbled,
> and whoever humbles
> himself will be exalted.

WWW.MATTHEW@23.12.NET

On that fateful day, I prayed a very simple prayer: *God strip me of all my preconceived notions of what this show should be—and please help me to just let go.* My friend Chris, who was present for that prayer, said he thought that that was what God was asking me to do—to just let Him take control and to watch and see how He would work things through.

I have always considered myself pretty creative, so letting go of that role and giving it over to the great Creator was a bit more challenging than I had imagined. Saying and doing are two profoundly different things.

The wheels of production began turning. An entire sound studio was placed on the rooftop of my loft in L.A. for a unique recording session of live musicians. Wild, visionary cameramen were hired, and big bucks were spent to make this program by the deadline set by my boss and the powers that be.

With all these things in motion and only a few days before we were to begin shooting, I realized that my mind had been stripped of everything I had imagined for this show. Suddenly I felt beyond ill equipped. *What on earth am I doing?* I thought as the clock ticked and the days of pre-production came to an end. My mentor and longtime friend Norm called me to check on our progress and to ask me what it was we were actually going to film. For the first time in a long time, my mind was completely empty of ideas. I feigned some sort of reasonable excuse for getting off the line with the promise that I would call him back and give him the details at a more convenient time (like when I had them).

There was not a plan in my head and only a day and a half to go before we began shooting the show. That night, the camera guys, who were famous for creating abstract visions and dreams, called to ask me what they would be shooting so they'd know what sort of props to bring. Once again, I scrambled for an excuse to call them back, promising that I would get them all the details they'd need, if they didn't mind a fax. They agreed.

I hung up feeling hung out—to dry.

Needless to say, this creator/director who had prayed to let go of all preconceived notions was now a rather clueless kind of guy. That is *so* not a good feeling. I had prayed that prayer rather innocently, thinking how great it would sound in the company of close friends to appear to let go of the biggest television opportunity I'd ever been entrusted with and give it all over to God to do as He saw fit.

NOW I FELT AS IF I SHOULD QUIT.

But later that night as I tossed and turned in fitful sleep, God pulled me up from a land of tortured dreams and had me fire up my laptop so He could write poetry through me. There, at about four in the morning above the breathtaking skyline of the City of Angels, five pages of a single-spaced television format in free verse came pouring through my keys. I watched the words fall out and float on my small computer screen. I wept as I read the words and then laughed because it all seemed so absurd. But through the laughter and tears, I knew that God had once again appeared in the final hour to give me everything I would need to make a program—His program—that would speak the language of a people in need.

I faxed the otherworldly script/poem to the camera crew, and later in the day I got a call from two guys who couldn't have been more excited by what they found waiting by their phone.

"We get it, James. We totally get it. We were crying while we read the fax, and we know exactly what you want to achieve."

I'm glad they knew what I wanted to achieve. I had simply asked to be stripped of all my ideas and move out to the dark land of believe. Apparently God had given me just what I needed to speak the language of the poetic dreamers who would bring this thing to life. God truly was directing; I was along for the ride.

When the guys showed up the next morning at 5 with a van loaded with unusual props, they informed me that they would shoot for 24 hours straight (I thought they were kidding) and handed me a breakdown of all our locations and how the shoot would go. I quickly realized that I, the creator/director (okay, so I was no longer the creator, but I was still the director), would be nowhere near the show. On nearly every shooting segment I was scheduled to be somewhere else, prepping for the next thing or sidelined or marginalized. "It makes no sense," I said to my friend Chris, "for the director to be so obviously pushed aside."

Chris just looked at me and smiled. "Isn't that what you asked for when we prayed the other day? That you would just let go? I think this may be an answer to your prayer. Remember: You wanted this to be God's show."

There is nothing worse than having people present when you ask God to do things that will strip you of your influence, prestige, and pride—unless it's having good friends side with strangers who ask you to step aside.

My only recourse was to ask God what I was supposed to do. *Cook,* He said.

FEED MY SHEEP.

The funny thing about God is that when you ask Him specific questions, He often surprises you with specific answers. I hadn't given food a thought, although every general and director knows that an army wins wars on full stomachs. So, instead of being a director, I went to the grocery store and bought a whole bunch of supplies to keep the troops happy while they traversed Los Angeles doing the drive-by shootings that would become the footage for this brand-new show.

As any of you who've worked in the film industry know, the director is basically the top of the food chain, while the person who makes and serves the food is way, way, way down the list as far as credits go. (I think the order might be different in God's programs.) As the hours ticked away, instead of throwing my weight around on the various sets and calling the shots, I found myself feeding our small army and washing a million pots.

Finally, around midnight, with prune-shriveled hands from the dishwater and smelling of smoke from having grilled fifty thousand assorted meats, I was shocked to learn that our amazing camera guys were vegetarians and that I had failed to provide them with something they could eat.

Utterly exhausted, I headed back to the kitchen to begin cooking again. I felt not at all like a director and not much like a chef. I fought hard not to collapse when I knelt down to serve the exhausted camera guys sitting cross-legged on the floor. They looked up and smiled. Those seekers, who didn't claim to know anything in particular about God, religion, or Jesus Christ, said something that night that forever changed my life.

"You know what has really impressed us about you?" they asked.

I thought for a moment. I knew it couldn't be my directing. And I was pretty sure it wasn't my cooking, because nothing I had cooked was meet for vegetarians. "No, I don't," I finally replied.

"We are blown away by how you were able to just let go

today—and then how you served."

I didn't know what to say, other than "thanks." I rushed back to the kitchen, claiming that I had forgotten the Parmesan cheese for their pasta. In the quiet of my kitchen, I realized what I had just learned. In the making of this important program for Him, God had revealed to me what is truly important in His kingdom:

> Humble yourselves in the sight of the Lord,
> and he shall lift you up.

WWW.JAMES@4.10.NET/KJV

The God of the universe had once let go of His role as the Great Director and robed Himself in the sweating, stinking flesh of man to show us heavenly things. This great God trudged the back deserts of the Middle East, giving up His right to create and direct and lord His position over us all. In the humility of a gentle carpenter and Savior, He let go and served. His letting go involved everything of importance, including His very life—a humble act of sacrifice that came at a hefty price.

The cost, however, has now been paid, and He's asking us to follow His lead in letting go and serving with our lives.

THE PRAYER OF J.BAEZ

I WILL NOT QUIT—UNTIL I'M THROUGH!

WHY DO WE BEGIN TO DIE
JUST BEFORE WE REACH THE OASIS?

There are places on this journey where the net of God's divine protection will surprise us when we least expect it but need it the most. If we are living this thing out the way we should—listening to the voice of the Father, moving in the power of the Holy Spirit, and expecting divine appointments or asking for them by name— we'll see Jesus move in us and through us, or in times of our own need, exquisitely on our behalf. That's exactly what happened to me the day Bruce Wilkinson, the author of *The Prayer of Jabez*, miraculously saved my life.

(TRUST ME: THIS MAN LIVES OUT WHAT HE WRITES.)

Shooting footage is only a small part of making television shows. The editing—piecing it all together—is often the toughest part, especially if you're doing nonlinear, reality-type TV. So, after my twenty-four-hour shooting spree (the one where I began to learn the lesson of "let go and serve"), I had to fly to Atlanta to begin the real work of putting the whole show together.

Our time line was so short that I didn't have time to view and log all the footage. I was sort of flying by the seat of my pants. But after seeing how powerfully God had moved in the L.A. portion of the show, I was confident that we were now good to go and that the minute I got to Atlanta the power of God would take hold of my mind and the program would come together in world-record time. FAT CHANCE

(LIKE WORLD-RECORD S L O W)   W

God had something else in mind for this particular leg of the journey. I expected the best, so I was ill prepared for the worst. The guys in Atlanta were top-notch TV pros who had chosen to "believe" a long time ago. The only problem was that they didn't necessarily believe in me, and when I showed them all my "amazing" footage, they didn't seem to like a thing they saw. "We have a lot of other footage you can use…if you want," Rick said sheepishly. "Feel free to look through our huge library."

S sHOT IN the FOOT-AGE.

As you walk out this journey called believe and venture into foreign lands filled with land mines, you will sometimes find your-self in places of desperate need. Some will be the result of your neglect—like forgetting to cover yourself with the full armor of God—and some will just be because you're in a battle with an enemy who's so much bigger than you. The other team will be extremely unhappy with the advances you're making or the threat you're posing, and you'll be pushed back by legions of hideous demons that want nothing more than to see you dead.

I'm not sure whether my neglect had anything to do with my losing battle in Atlanta, but I do know that I was making a tele-vision pilot that had the potential to touch lives around the world. The format was fresh and inviting, and the message was one of great hope for people who would never walk through the doors of a church. It was an exciting assignment—until the legions from hell came knocking at my hotel door.

I THOUGHT IT WAS ROOM SERVICE....

(HOW NICE—COULD YOU BRING ME A BIT MORE ICE?)

Since Satan is the prince of the power of the air, there are some who believe that when you dabble in the media (**air**waves) with a message that actually matters, you are simply asking for trouble. That may sound spooky and Perretti-esque, but the simple fact of the matter is that I lived it, and it was the most hellish experience of my life. And even though the like-minded television visionaries in Atlanta were amazing guys, they didn't seem to see what I was seeing in the footage I needed them to assemble.

FENDING OFF FRIENDLY FIRE.

Frankly, there is nothing more discouraging than having members of your own team think you're nuts. It's tough enough when the other team thinks you've lost the plot, but when your teammates are questioning your sanity, it's a whole other kind of discouragement.

The editing process became mind-numbingly difficult. I had a total of eleven days set aside, with a nonchangeable, nonrefundable plane ticket that would whisk me back to L.A. with or without a finished show. We were on a tight deadline and an even tighter budget, and everything depended on my finishing this project in the allotted time. I had to be on a plane and out of Atlanta come hell or high water. Hell and high water both came, and I began to boil while drowning in the heated flood.

Five days into the project we had approximately a minute and a half of show laid to tape and six days left to assemble the remaining twenty-seven and a half minutes. If you do the math, you'll quickly see that things were even more desperate than I'm leading you to believe. If it was going to take five days for less than two minutes of show, I would need a few dozen weeks in Atlanta to finish it off.

COULD I BORROW SOMEBODY'S PROZAC, PAXIL, OR EXTRA-STRENGTH ZOLOFT?

At the end of each frenzied day, I would go back to my hotel and sweat and pace the floor. I would find that, despite the fact that I was working fifteen- and seventeen-hour days, I just couldn't sleep because of the anxiety produced by knowing how much was riding on the success of this show. There would never be enough days to finish, no matter how hard I shouted "in Jesus' name" in my room at night.

ALL ALONE.

On day six I was nearly about to die from exhaustion and the very real creeping feeling of insanity. I don't believe I've ever come that close to the brink, even though I always seem to be riding life way too close to the edge.

"I KISS THE EDGES WITH MY TOES."
R I V E R   P H O E N I X

(UNFORTUNATELY FOR HIM, THE EDGES KISSED BACK.)

And it felt like the edge was about to engage me in a big, wet Judas kiss of death. I stepped into the production house in a complete stupor. I know my eyes had a crazy, glassy look when I bumped into Bruce Wilkinson. (For the life of me, I still don't really know why he was there.)

🐛 A.D.D. JEALOUSY

I really hate to admit this, but if it weren't for the fact that Bruce saved my life the first time we met, I might have wanted to bump him off my publisher's roster. He's selling six billion more books than I am, and everywhere I go someone asks me, "Have you read *The Prayer of Jabez*?" I smile—politely, because it's an amazing book that's changing lives around the world. But truth be told, I wanted to be the author that was being treated like a king.

(I'M PRETTY SURE THAT'S WHY GOD PICKED BRUCE INSTEAD OF ME.)

If you haven't read *The Prayer of Jabez,* you're not only in the minority, but you're also missing out on a great little book with a powerful, life-changing message. Rather than give the whole book's premise away (although I'd probably sell a lot more books that way), suffice it to say that if you pray along the lines of this little prayer, you'll undoubtedly find yourself in unbelievable, divine appointments where God will do miracles in the lives of those you meet, simply because you asked. The day I met Bruce must have been one of the eleven thousand days or so that he has asked.

I was on the edge of disaster, dancing dangerously with defeat, so I walked up boldly and introduced myself. "Hi, Bruce, I'm James. And I have a very important question." (At the time I didn't realize that Bruce was in the business of keeping divine appointments.)

"What can I do for you, James?" he asked.

"Bruce, I was wondering…. When you are working on a project that has the potential to really have an impact on the world, do you ever find yourself under massive attack in the spiritual realm?" This kind of understatement isn't even like me, but the panic on my face and in my general demeanor screamed out on my behalf, underlining and highlighting my question in ways that a man of God like Bruce could clearly see.

"James," Bruce began, "if you are doing something that has great potential to make a real and tangible difference, there are times when the warfare feels so intense that you think you might actually die." I breathed a huge sigh of relief. He had said what I had been afraid to say out loud.

But then he went over that edge—and I didn't even push him.

"Not only that, but I bet you're finding that the name of Jesus is doing absolutely no good at all."

HERESY!
THAT NAME IS THE MOST POWERFUL NAME OF ALL.

When he said those words, I completely fell apart. "How did you know? I was shouting Jesus' name till four o'clock in the morning, and it was about as helpful as the name Bozo. What's up with that?"

Bruce smiled as he stepped closer to explain in a warm, fatherly sort of way. The Bozo thing was probably a little much for him, but he chalked it up to my temporary insanity, I'm sure.

"James, this has nothing to do with the name of Jesus. This has everything to do with you and your tenacity. The enemy is trying to get you to quit. He wants you to fail, and he wants you to believe that you are going to fail so you'll give up."

"I know, Bruce. Last night I said that as soon as this is over, I'm going to give up my career in television and start working at Starbucks."

Bruce laughed. Looking into my eyes, he continued: "That is exactly what the enemy wanted you to say. You spoke out exactly what he wanted. Now, I'm going to show you how to lift this heaviness from you by speaking out what God wants you to say. Are you ready?"

I was dying to hear what Bruce was about to tell me. And dying because I didn't already know. "James, I want you to say these words out loud: **I will not quit until this project is complete.**"

I smiled vaguely.

"Now say it, James."

"I will not quit until this project is complete," I repeated.

KaBam!

In that very instant the heaviness lifted and 3,000 high-intensity lights came on in my dark soul.

"Say it again." Bruce looked stern now. I said it three more times, just to make sure.

As crazy as this may sound, I experienced instant relief—something so profound and real and electric that I began laughing out loud.

SATAN HAS LEFT THE BUILDING.

As I walked back into the edit bay with new vigor and fortitude and resolve, I muttered over and over under my breath, "I will not quit—until I'm through."

The very night Bruce saved my life, we broke the sound barrier—I think we might even have edged close to the speed of light—as we busted out nearly eight and a half minutes of show before we left that place. In the five remaining days, we were working so many hours that there was no extra time to prepare for the upcoming day, but God worked around that hurdle in a miraculous way. He woke me every morning at approximately 3 A.M. to give me a list of the edits for the next day's session.

There's so much more I could tell you about what God did to get His show on the road, but the most important lesson I learned in Atlanta is that when God sends you to do an impossible job, He wants you to trust Him to bring you through. And if you falter in the area of trust and begin filling out an application at the nearest Starbucks, well…then He may send in the reinforcements in the form of His net, His network of empowered believers who actually believe that God will speak if they are listening and are willing to be used.

In my case, God sent in one of the best, and I'll forever be grateful for Bruce and the now-famous prayer of Jabez. Eight months later, at a special dinner for Multnomah authors in New Orleans, I walked up to Bruce and thanked him again for having taken time out of his schedule to save my life on that horrific day in Atlanta. He looked a bit puzzled at first, but then I saw a glimmer of recognition cross his face.

"Oh, yes," he said, "I remember now. It was my pleasure, and

I'm glad God used me to help." The top brass of the company were listening in, probably in an effort to protect their star player from being exposed to the likes of me.

"And I just wanted to tell you, Bruce," I went on, "I really loved *The Prayer of Joan Baez*—what a powerful, powerful book!" (I keep a very straight face when I joke like this.)

For a moment it was as if time stood still. A look of complete bewilderment crossed Bruce's face, and the heads of the company held their collective breath, not knowing what Bruce might do. Then, without a word, Bruce reached into his jacket.

(I THOUGHT THAT PERHAPS HE NOW REGRETTED HIS LIFESAVING GESTURE AND WAS GOING TO CAP ME WITH A SMALL 9MM.)

But he pulled out a small notepad as he burst into laughter. "Oh, I've got to remember that one," he chuckled. "The Prayer of Joan Baez!" And he jotted it down in his little book.

I don't know for sure what he's going to do with that absurd little tidbit I gave him, but I know what I did with the lifesaving one he gave me. I used it to finish an incredible, God-breathed show before my 6 A.M. flight back to the City of Angels. And I used it to let the rest of the world know that Bruce Wilkinson is a man true to the words he penned in the incredible little book that is touching the lives of millions. Thanks, Bruce.

I will not quit—until I'm through.

Now I'm using that on almost everything I do. I've even used it on this book a time or two.

> We do not want you to be uninformed, brothers,
> about the hardships we suffered in [the desert]. We were under
> great pressure, far beyond our ability to endure, so that we despaired
> even of life. Indeed, in our hearts we felt the sentence of death.
> But this happened that we might not rely
> on ourselves but on God, who raises the dead.
>
> WWW.2CORINTHIANS@1.8–9.NET

DIE AND LET LIVE

GOD NOSE

—IT TAKES PRACTICE GETTING PAST THE STENCH OF DEATH AND THOSE UNFASHIONABLE GRAVE CLOTHES!

On this journey through the desert of the real, there are some real dangers that we all have to face.

LIKE THE PRACTICE OF DEATH.

Sometimes it's real death, but more often it's death to a vision or a dream. If anything, even a God-breathed thing, becomes more important than God, that thing will have to die—as crazy as it seems. Because God is not as worried about our visions and dreams as He is about our desire to continue to trust and follow Him, even when the words He has spoken don't materialize in the way or at the time we imagine. This might make us think that it was all imagined. But the truth is simply this: In God's reality, death always precedes new life. New life can come only after real death. For many of us on this journey beyond belief, death isn't a part of our itinerary. Nevertheless, it is a part of God's

HIDDEN AGENDA.

During the final days of editing the program in Atlanta, just after the madness faded and clarity broke through, God began waking me every night between 3 and 5 A.M. to tell me certain things—to instruct me about the next day's edits or simply to ask me to pray. God knows it was tough enough on four to five hours of sleep every night, so His wake-up calls were maybe not as welcome as I'd like you to think.

PLEASE DO NOT DISTURB.

But it became clear that God was doing some astounding things as He walked me through the final stages of the show. He had truly taken me up on my dumb prayer to "let go." I was on the edge, but He was clearly in charge, giving me everything I needed to see this program through.

Then, on one of my final nights in my lonely hotel in Atlanta, God woke me to alert me to something that He was about to do. He was about to bring death once again—death to my vision and all the dreams I had for this unusual show. And for the life of me, it's so hard to understand why He wanted me to know

AT 3 A.M.!

That particular night I was more exhausted than usual. I had put in around eighteen hours in the edit bay and desperately needed sleep and inspiration to finish on time. But right around

3 A.M.—just a few short hours into my sleep—God seemed to shout at me to get to my feet and pray. I was baffled. The last thing I needed (I thought) was to have to get out of bed and have profound things to say.

But God let me know that the prayer wasn't for me; it was for my boss, friend, and mentor Norm, the programming head. He answered directly to the president and had been responsible for bringing me on board. *Why in the world do I have to pray for Norm?* I thought. *Shouldn't he be praying for me? I'm getting no sleep, my nerves are frayed, and this program will be finished only by a divine act of alchemy!* But God let me know that Norm was in trouble and that I needed to pray for him. After a brief, dazed argument, I got out of bed and began to lift up my friend. Then I went back to bed.

Later that day I called Norm's secretary and asked how he was doing. I explained that I had been awakened in the middle of the night to pray on his behalf. Through tears and stuttered words, Sandy told me the other half: Norm had been let go. He was no longer my boss, and I was still carrying this ridiculous cross. Something told me through this horrible news that no matter how powerful this program might turn out to be, it too would die before it was born.

A TIME TO LAUGH,
A TIME TO MOURN.

And to tell you the truth, I did laugh. I laughed at the absurdity of the situation. I laughed because sometimes it's just too hard to cry when the only question that keeps going through your troubled mind is:

Why, God, why?

I also had to mourn, because I was so looking forward to this program—this vision, this dream, this baby being born. And I had to cry for my good friend Norm. I had been so certain that God had brought this whole thing about and that He was going to do miraculous things with it...not kill it.

It's funny, this death thing. Even Jesus experienced a similar set of circumstances.

Jesus loved Martha and her sister and Lazarus.
Yet when he heard that Lazarus was sick,
he stayed where he was two more days.

WWW.JOHN@11.5–6.NET

When Jesus was told that His best friend Lazarus was sick unto death, He set the unusual example of "die and let live." Instead of heading right out and healing his buddy, He hung around and seemed to His disciples to be acting a bit nutty. But what they didn't know was that He was up to something far more miraculous than a simple healing. God was about to do some powerful new dealing, and His cards would reveal that death was merely the beginning of new life for those willing to hang on to belief—for those willing to get past the stench of the grave and the grave sense of grief. Remember: Jesus set the example for us to follow, and sometimes His way seems a bit tough to swallow.

JESUS SAID:

"Lazarus is dead, and for your sake I am glad I was not there,
so that you may believe. But let us go to him."
Then Thomas…said to the rest of the disciples,
"Let us also go, that we may die with him."

WWW.JOHN@11.14–16.NET

In this particular case, Thomas wasn't doubting, and I believe that's exactly what we are called to do—not doubt. Go and die with Him. Die and let live so new life may begin.

Look at the historical record. So many of God's promises first faced death. He had promised Abraham that he would be the father of a nation, and when that miracle occurred—when that son Isaac was finally born—God did something so absurd that Abraham's heart had to be torn. God asked him to take his son's life on the side of a mountain with a very sharp knife.

INHUMAN SACRIFICE.

What kind of God would ask a thing like that? What kind of
Father would require another father to perform something so horrific—something so much against the rules of his God? Maybe
only a Father who would ask nothing less of Himself. God allowed
His only Son to come to earth to fulfill the promise of eternal life
and redemption in a whole new dimension, but only after facing
death Himself. It doesn't make a whole lot of sense—until you
realize that if God makes the rules, God can break the rules and
work outside the natural while He dabbles in the supernatural to
remind us of a most important point: just TrUst.

"Lord," Martha said to Jesus, "if you had been here, my brother would
not have died…. Jesus said to her, "I am the resurrection and the life.
He who believes in me will live, even though he dies;
and whoever lives and believes in me will never die. Do you believe this?"

WWW.JOHN@11.21–26.NET

I tried to believe this as I scrambled to finish the program in
the face of this death, and I let God know that no matter what, I
wasn't going to quit until I was through—until His program was
finished.

IT IS FINISHED.

No matter what happened around me, no matter how the
other team tried to confound me, I wanted to continue to believe

that God was going to bring life to my friend. I wanted to trust and believe for new life again. And I wanted to believe that some-day, somehow, this program would accomplish not what I wanted to do, but what God would intend, just as he did for dead Lazarus—just what He did for His friend. **HE WEPT.**

What a powerful and telling moment. The God who could do anything at all, including raising the dead, allowed His human-ity to show through the tears that He shed. He cried. I can't exactly figure it all out, knowing that He knew everything, including how this episode would end. But I know this: He chose to weep for the loss of His friend even though He knew that the loss would soon end. I don't think it's such a bad thing to let your humanity show. Tears seem to water the soul. And when we are willing to simply let go and mourn our loss, we can see the hope of a new beginning on the other side of our cross.

JESUS AGAIN:

"Take away the stone," he said. "But, Lord," said Martha, the sister of the dead man, "by this time there is a bad odor, for he has been there four days." Then Jesus said, "Did I not tell you that if you believed, you would see the glory of God?" So they took away the stone. Then Jesus looked up and said, "Father, I thank you that you have heard me. I knew that you always hear me, but I said this for the benefit of the people standing here,

that they may believe that you sent me." When he had said this, Jesus

called in a loud voice, "Lazarus, come out!" The dead man came out, his

hands and feet wrapped with strips of linen, and a cloth around his face.

Jesus said to them, "Take off the grave clothes and let him go."

WWW.JOHN@11.39–44.NET

Jesus did all this so the world would know that He trusted His Father to finish the work. It wasn't His magic or charisma, and He wasn't a cult leader gone berserk. He was God's Son, willing to trust beyond a very real death and a very real grave, foreshadowing a very personal resurrection for a world that He would save.

Perhaps Jesus had to believe for a friend before He could do it for Himself. For one day He would be pushed to that ultimate place of trust—where He would have to lay His life down on that old rugged cross, where He would bleed and believe that His Father would be good as His word and not abandon His Son, but empower Him with new life again (despite the smell and a visit to a very real hell). That may take some practice—even for Jesus—and I suspect that it takes even more practice for people like us to move in that place of complete and total TRUST.

TRUST.

A ROSE AGAIN

That ill-fated show—**"The Rest"**—met its demise at the hands of the network heads. It all happened so fast.

So long. Not so long ago.

REST IN PEACE.

Rest. That is really all God wants from us anyway: to let go of everything we think we need, everything we think we know, and trust beyond what we can see into the dark land of believe. Into the land where God alone can see. Into His eternity. And when we enter that place of rest, we can sleep, nestled close to the One who has given life to our dreams—the One who bought life for the rest because of His death.

As outrageous as all of this may seem, I believe that God simply wants us to trust Him with all of our visions and all of our dreams—to trust Him with our lives on this journey beyond belief. In this place of trust we come to understand our real roles as sons and daughters in His great plan. We aren't accomplishing anything

He couldn't accomplish for Himself. So many of us are concerned with our success, our health, and our wealth so we can continue to do and do and do for our God, when all He's really asking is for us to trust Him and let go.

HOW ODD.

One of my final wake-up calls in Atlanta (before the angel of death visited this great little show) involved God asking me to get on-line and apply for a rose. He said that it was time to submit this program to the festival in Switzerland, The Golden Rose, so He could fulfill a promise He'd made a long, long time ago in a reality far away—the promise He'd made when I lived down under after giving my old life away.

I was pretty sure we had missed the deadline, but I listened and obeyed. I found the submission forms on-line, and God's timing was such that with the help of Federal Express, "The Rest" would arrive on the cutoff day.

I MUST ADMIT THAT I WAS TRULY AMAZED.

God was asking me to believe. I sent the program just as my job came to an end. God's little baby was now in a basket of reeds flying high in the heavens over land, over sea. With tight finances and no job on the horizon, I couldn't even figure out how I could afford to go to a ridiculously expensive country just on the off chance that we would win an award.

I ASKED FOR A MIRACLE.

God is really full of surprises. Not only was the program nominated for a Golden Rose, but a phone call came when I was about to bail out on the whole big event because of all the money that would have to be spent: LODGING, FOOD, AND A FLIGHT (TO EUROPE, NO LESS). It was a festival organizer inviting me to serve as a judge on the prestigious international jury. He called rather late, so I would really have to hurry to book a flight. But the jurors would be given four-star hotel accommodations and more meals than anyone needed or should eat, just for sitting for several hours in one semicomfortable seat—judging.

God continued to provide. I found ridiculously cheap tickets on the Internet, and my **jury duty** ensured that all my other major expenses were met, so I was free to attend the awards. I was free to go and believe that God would make good on the word He had delivered to a land down under so many years before. What would this second trip to Switzerland have in store?

Ironically, I had been asked to serve on the music jury—the very jury that would judge my entry. I wasn't sure if that was good or bad, but I figured the show would have at least one vote that way.

WRONG AGAIN.

Because my program had been nominated and I was serving on the jury, there was no end of jealousy and animosity. A rule was made forbidding me from voting on my own program or from even being in the room while it was being shown. During the days leading up to the viewing, the other jurors were leery of me, suspicious that my friendly nature was just a ploy to get their votes. It was the worst possible scenario, and instead of seeing a golden rose, I began to see red.

After the jury viewed "The Rest," they let me back in. Before that, they'd been colder than ice; now everyone was syrupy nice. The friendly warmth that filled the room came from their decision to disqualify my program because it wasn't exactly a music program.

"It really has a format all its own," the chief juror said to me as if he were throwing me a bone. "We are so sorry. It really shouldn't have been entered in this category.

"Exactly what category should it have been entered in?" I asked, ready again to rear my ugly, prideful head—the one that should have died on the last ill-fated Golden Rose trip.

"Hard to say…. Your show is truly groundbreaking and unique. It's like nothing we've ever seen."

With that, the discussion was over, and the hope for a rose

died again. I don't know how many deaths that made. I had quit counting. And I was about to quit counting on the word of my Friend. But then I remembered: The word from my God so many years ago was that I would win a Golden Rose for Best Human Values. Looking past the death knell sounded by the music jury, I held on to that final hope.

I went back to my room and began cleaning my house. I asked God to take away my frustration and the anger I felt toward the jurors who had dealt me that blow. I asked to love and live in peace and continue to show Jesus even if I didn't win a Golden Rose—to share life and goodness and hope with the people I met and to be Jesus with skin on, whatever the festival's outcome.

It made a world of difference from the other time I attended. I felt God's very real peace wash over me and through me as I loved all the people I met on the floor. I didn't care so much about the golden trophy, which had been so tempting all those years ago. And there was joy—joy that was bigger and more important than an international award because it was born in God's Word. We have a choice—one we must learn to make no matter how we feel, no matter what's at stake.

I chose to believe again. I believed what my God had said: He was going to give me a rose. Every time I passed that crystal case that held the four-thousand-dollar trophies, I claimed the one that

had the dove. It was the rose for the program with the Best
Human Values, the rose that celebrates love. I knew that my God
had spoken and that the dove was like the one for dear old Noah.
It was my symbol of hope and a symbol of the spirit of the award
itself—of peace, forgiveness, love, gentleness, and turning the other
cheek. I began to reach out to the same people that had brought
me no end of grief.

Finally, the big night arrived. A good friend who had helped
work on the show took a train from Paris to be there that night. As
we put on our tuxedos, we prayed for God's will to be done. No
matter what happened, we were determined to have a whole lot of
fun. I mean, how often do you even get nominated for an international award in television? How often does the Swiss government
subsidize a four-star hotel and a ton of great meals? (More cheese
than I ever hope to see again in this lifetime, but I'm not complaining. Those Swiss have something different in mind when they
talk about wheels.)

After spending some time in the huge hall filled with big
cheeses and international television professionals from dozens of
countries, I decided to slip off to the bathroom for a moment of
relief. As I was washing my face, Antonio, one of my fellow jurors
(the most annoying of anyone on my team and the one I had to
work the hardest to love), ran up to me and threw his arms around

me in a hard and crazy hug.

UN-TIMELY A.D.D. MOMENT

Being hugged in a men's bathroom by someone
you don't particularly like is disconcerting. But when
that person delivers a rose with the hug, you quickly forget
the setting and hug back with all your might.
(I think we scared a few of the more conservative Swiss types.)

Antonio broke the rules of the international jury by letting me
know that I might want to prepare a speech, for in a few short
moments a Golden Rose would be within my reach. He let me
know that "The Rest" had won a Rose d'Or, or a Golden Rose for
Best Human Values. I could barely speak and was extremely grateful that my new friend had given me time to recuperate and prepare. Soon, I would be on a world stage where I would have a
chance to share my thanks to my God, my very best Friend, for
allowing me to see His promise come to be—in spite of the desert,
the hardship, and those stupid dancing fleas.

ON THE OTHER SIDE OF DEATH,
ON THE OTHER SIDE OF DEFEAT,
GOD DELIVERS ON HIS WORD
FOR THOSE WILLING TO BELIEVE.

The lessons that I learned this time—the lesson to hold on to God's Word and continue to believe despite obvious defeat, the lesson to love Antonio and turn the other cheek—allowed me to see another miracle delivered by my Friend. He saw the end from the beginning, and I saw Him deliver on His promise in the end—five years later…

A ROSE AGAIN

PART- III

A FISH STORY

Jesus said, "Come, follow me, and I will make you fishers of men." And just before He was taken up into heaven, He told us to go into all the world and make disciples of all nations. Although we should be fishing for men all the time on this journey beyond belief, I think most of us make the decision to believe and then go on vacation. Every single trip we make is a mission trip—to Siberia or across the street.

I'm no expert, but I've seen a lot of fishing expeditions that do more to scare the fish than reel them in. I believe we've been doing this all wrong—casting our nets on the wrong side while allowing our preconceived notions and stupid pride to rob the lost of God's message of exquisite life, here and on the other side. To be effective fisherman, we need to learn the language of the tribes we try to reach, including the one that may be living on our street. As we move in love—listening while fishing—in time, we will see God supernaturally fill our nets.

Dawson Trotman said, "If you're re not fishing, it's questionable how close you are following." Are you following Jesus?

THEN LET'S GO FISH!

CASTING CALL

LISTEN TO THE MASTER,
AND YOUR NETS WILL BE FULL FASTER.

Go therefore and make disciples of all nations, baptizing them in the
name of the Father and the Son and the Holy Spirit, teaching them to
observe all that I commanded you.

WWW.MATTHEW@28.19-20.NET/NASB

Making it through the desert is one important part of following Jesus on this journey beyond belief. But there is more to it than
just endurance, trust, and perseverance. If we want to have a role
on Jesus' stage, we have to show up at His casting call and be
assigned our parts to play. Throughout our lives, we'll all play the
part of a fisherman, because before leaving the scene, Jesus said
that we are to go and make disciples of all nations. We are, in fact,
to become fishers of men.

Although the Master commissioned us to go out and fill our
nets with the lost and dying to prevent a mass exodus to hell, we've
done a terrible job of fishing for men. Nobody likes to be told,
"You're doing it wrong." It just sort of rubs us the wrong way. Our

pride tends to rear its ugly head, and we come up with 50 million reasons why we are, in fact, doing it the right way. It's even worse when that something is our profession, or our calling. But if you look at our nets and the extent of our catch, you can see that no matter how professional we may think we are, we are very far from seeing what God can really do.

Peter was a fisherman by profession. Most good fishermen I've met seem like some of the most prideful men—in that good old American sort of prideful way—and I'm guessing it may not have been much different in Jesus' day. Peter probably didn't like being told he was doing it the wrong way.

Imagine the scene…. Jesus' disciples were pretty bummed out; their teacher and Savior had been publicly humiliated and murdered right before their eyes. All they had given themselves to over the past few years now seemed like just a pack of lies. Now what on earth could they possibly do—try to win converts to some dead, deluded Jew? There really was only one thing to do, and that was to return to what they knew.

GO FISH!

So Peter and several others stripped down to nearly nothing as they usually did and tried to catch some fish. But they toiled unsuccessfully in their old career. In the middle of their fruitless endeavor, a voice from shore asked them if they'd caught anything.

I've fished only a handful of times, but every time I have, a stranger has ambled by and asked that same innocent question. But this question wasn't innocent, and it was not a random stranger. In fact, the situation couldn't have been any stranger: A dead guy just happened by to ask how the fishing has been. And, then, in the next breath, He had the nerve to tell them they were doing it all wrong.

JESUS...

"Children, you do not have any fish, do you?" They answered Him, "No." And He said to them, "Cast the net on the right-hand side of the boat and you will find a catch." So they cast, and then they were not able to haul it in because of the great number of fish.

WWW.JOHN@21.5–6.NET/NASB

When Peter realized that it was Jesus giving the fishing lesson, he suddenly felt naked and exposed and threw on all his clothes, only to jump in the water. I would think he'd take off his clothes to jump in the water, but I'm guessing that the clothes were just a cover-up and that he may have used the water to disappear. Because this little fishing trip was just another sign of unbelief and fear, and Peter was undoubtedly feeling a bit ashamed, since he had already denied that he even knew Jesus' name.

Jesus had just risen from the dead, and He appeared to seven of His downtrodden disciples (who had abandoned their mission to go back to fishin') to tell them that, even though they were fisher-men by trade, they were doing it wrong. Jesus was not afraid to point this out. In fact, He probably had to shout, "Hey, you're doing that wrong…throw your nets on the other side if you want to catch some fish." Jesus didn't micromanage much while He walked the earth, and He didn't reprimand the disciples for going back to their old ways. He just pointed out that they were doing the old thing in a bad way and then offered some fishing tips.

All of this seems a bit fishy if you really think about it. Jesus commanded us all to become fishers of men, but the only time He really told us how was after He came back from the dead. In this strange story, one of the first things Jesus did on the other side of the grave was to tell His followers to throw their net on the other side of the boat if they wanted to see a catch that would take them aback.

The lesson seems almost ludicrous. The boats they used for fishing were very small, and if the net was on one side or the other wouldn't seem to matter at all. As silly as it seems, though, I'm guessing that the lesson was extra important, since after Jesus rose from the dead, it was one of the first things He said.

Even now, as I think about this strange tale, I wonder what the most sublime meaning of "cast your net on the other side" could be. Since I'm probably missing the real supernatural subtext,

I'm going with the obvious moral of this fish story: In fishing for men, we've been fishing on the wrong side of the boat.

I recently learned that despite all our technology and worldwide media coverage, the number of those who claim to believe is actually less (in overall percentages) than it was one hundred years ago. Whatever our profession and however good our intentions, we're clearly doing a pretty lame job of bringing in the fish.

In an attempt to understand on which side of the boat our nets should be, let's take a quick look at the side we're familiar with. It seems that we have our nets where most of the fish have already been caught. We put our money and our time in the places where we as Christians all feel the safest—in large and luxurious buildings where we can talk freely of things that mean nothing to those most in need. We talk about blessing, redemption, and sanctified lives. We mention fellowship and cell groups and God-fearing wives. We hold revivals and potlucks and singles retreats, while the rest of the world just dies in the streets.

We've spent billions of dollars building huge cathedrals, temples, and churches; we've spent even more on satellites, television studios, and make-up artists to make up for the absence of artists and the artistry of loving and empowered fishers of men. We've taken a stunning message of beauty and turned it into a boring, banal message about mere morality. Or, if we haven't focused on rigid rules, we've made ourselves look like fools bouncing up and down like a bunch of clowns asking a doubtful, dying world for even more money so we can continue to fish on the wrong side of the boat by bringing the message to the masses who already know and in a language only they know.

What corporation or business do you know of that can have consistent losses and zero growth and continue to justify spending more money to keep these sinking cathedrals afloat?

Jesus Himself gave us a mandate to go out and spread this news to those who are living and dying in sin—to those who are in bondage to fear and addiction. He commands us to live like we mean it by allowing the news that has changed us to become the news that will change them, when they witness the change that has come over us and overcome us with a love that flows through us and a joy that's infectious. If we want to see our nets fill until they are breaking, it may be time to take Jesus' advice:

"CAST YOUR NETS ON THE OTHER SIDE!"

I have an incredible new group of friends who desire to reach our dying world in a powerful new way. They spend most of their nonworking, waking hours ministering on the street. Not in the old fashioned way—screaming Scriptures from soapboxes to a passing crowd. These guys would never be that loud. They are under-the-radar Christians who go wherever God leads. While going about their everyday lives, they keep listening to the things their God is saying, and when the time is right and God prompts them to move, they share what He says with whomever He chooses.

One of the guys is a former Marine who has become a most potent killing machine. (When I say killing, I'm referring to the kingdom of darkness—members of the opposing team.) Over the years God has stripped Jared of everything that once gave him strength, and now in his weakness he moves in power, using every chance he gets to help point the people he meets back to the Master.

Jared recently told me the story of how he'd been hit by a truck. He was pretty much disabled, had no insurance, and was completely out of money—seemingly out of luck. In that place of pain and defeat, he humbly made his way to the office of Dr. Larry in the hope that he would be a good doctor who would work out a deal to help a broken man heal.

Larry was in fact a good doctor, but he was a bad man in a whole mess of trouble. While Jared was vulnerable on a rolling table, loosening His muscles, God was loosening his tongue. And before he knew what was happening, he was telling Larry all the things that were going on in the doctor's life   things that had Dr. Larry speechless until Jared realized that he had been speaking for nearly thirty minutes and stopped.

Then Larry asked, "Who are you, and how do you know these things?"

"I am a servant of the Most High God," Jared replied, "and He told me these things."

In a short amount of time, Dr. Larry chose to believe. It didn't take some well-crafted sermon or a great amount of prep and worry. God simply chose to appear and speak through a servant who was willing to be open and obedient. Now, several years later, this same doctor has led nearly fifty other people to the amazing God who speaks. How many have those fifty touched on their own journeys beyond belief?

Jared has a million of these stories—like the time he picked up a hitchhiker who, it turned out, had a gun. My friend realized that he was about to be molested and murdered. "That was not the way I was going to go out," he said. So he began to pray in the Spirit right there in front of his assailant. Jared said that after only a few seconds the criminal blacked out—some would say from the Spirit, others might claim from fear—but whatever the case, when the man came to, he was dumfounded and unwilling to carry out his former plan. Instead, he asked, "Who are you?"

"I'm a servant and a son of the Most High God," Jared replied.

Immediately the man began to confess. He said that he'd been living a heinous life of sin and that he'd planned to make my friend just another statistic on that L.A. summer night. He claimed that he'd been chased for many years by very real demons and was tired of his crazy life. Over dinner recently, Jared told me how that man allowed Jesus into his heart, gave up his evil ways, and made a brand-new start.

I can't prove that Jared's stories are true. But on three separate occasions I've heard him say things about me, my friends, and strangers that he never could have known on his own. They weren't vague and simple things like a horoscope that could apply to several scenarios in several different ways. They were words so specific and so on target that I thought about them for days.

BY THEIR FRUIT YOU WILL RECOGNIZE THEM....

My good friend Norm, the guy who lost his job during the making of "The Rest," had come to the end of his rope after spending more than a year looking for a new career. Jared invited him to his house for a time of prayer. He let Norm know that God was completely aware of his situation and that within three weeks there would be a massive breakthrough. But first there would be a week of rest. Jared said, "Just watch what God is going to do."

Jared didn't know it, but Norm had already planned to take his family on vacation during spring break—the very next week. Without a shred of hope on the horizon and only the words of his

God to stand on, Norm chose to believe. And three weeks later, almost to the day, Norm was hired to be the head of a communication program at a graduate school out East. There really isn't much more to say. These things happen when you allow God to speak and live like you believe.

Even though these things aren't as evident as they used to be in the lives of many who claim to believe, it isn't too late or too hard to get them back. All we need to do is ask. And when these fruits of the Spirit are evident in our lives, much will be said on Jesus' behalf without our speaking a single word.

If you are at all like me, you've probably been a witness to the travesties that have been done in the name of "witnessing." When I was a kid, our little church would go out on Wednesday nights, knocking on doors to spread the light. I think we did more to spread the fright. Quite frankly, people are pretty much freaked out by door-to-door anythings, but especially door-to-door fanatics who want to sell Jesus like a multilevel marketing scheme. Maybe back in Little-House-on-the-Prairie days that sort of thing was effective, but today people are so skeptical that door-to-door evangelism—even preaching on the streets—is so ineffective that I think even Jesus weeps.

I think that the way we've been representing the greatest message the world could ever hear has, for the most part, made our job much harder. I think we've used a prosperity message that doesn't quite pan out, or we've used tactics laced with fear. If we haven't succumbed to those devices, we've used canned scripts as our bait to catch fish. Do we fish or cut bait?

WHAT ABOUT LOVE?

Jesus said, "They will know you are Christians by your love." But if we were to poll the average person on the street, I'd bet that the first word they'd associate with Christians wouldn't be *love*. Most people I've spoken to focus on the hate—the hate we have for homos, abortionists, Democrats, and freaks. Whatever happened to *turn the other cheek?*

Jesus never spewed words of hate to those in so much need. It was for the hookers, lepers, and sinners that His hands and feet would bleed—the very ones He had often helped to feed.

AN A.D.D. MOMENT

Growing up, I went to a church where women couldn't
wear makeup or be caught dead wearing pants
(now there's an interesting picture). Movies were a terrible sin,
as was any sort of movement that could be considered a dance.
When a visitor would come in through the doors—someone who
may have been in serious need—all eyes would notice the list
of infractions the poor sinner had committed before he even
made it to the pew. I'm still asking God to help me let go
of my anger for the things that Christians would often do—
things I still often do (like judge).

I believe that the first step in becoming powerful fishers of
men is to ask God to fill us with a His supernatural love for those
in desperate need. Love is not something that comes naturally to
us, and yet God can do mighty things through it when we allow it
to live in us and flow through us.

> And this is His commandment: that we should believe
> on the name of His Son Jesus Christ and love one another.

WWW.1JOHN@3.23.NET/NKJV

Like most things on this journey beyond belief, it all begins
with ask. And then we are to love and listen while we go to the
other side and cast. And while we are fishing, we need to keep

listening to the voice of the Creator for the words of life that He will speak through us to them—the unlikely, the doctors, the molesters, the business executives—in order to see real miracles begin. Then just watch the fish come in.

A FISH STORY

DEep-sEe FISHING
DIVE RIGHT IN, AND
LOVE THE SINNER,
~~HATE THE SIN.~~

The god of this world has blinded
the minds of the unbelieving that they might not see.
WWW.2CORINTHIANS@4.4.NET/NASB

When I was a child, dreams of flight robbed me of many nights of sleep. I remember the almost autistic repetition of those flying dreams. My subconscious brain waves leaked a secret of the universe, a brilliant key to unlock the door of flight. This is a secret I will now openly share: We don't need an airship or a waxen set of wings; we are designed by God to fly. But very few discover this truth because few will ever try.

FEW WILL EVER DIVE.

The closest a person can come to actual flying is an incredible aquatic sport called scuba diving. Lulled by the rhythmic, regulated breathing of your self-contained air supply, you glide weightless over mountainous underwater formations, cresting sheer rock cliffs, while your stomach drops and your heart races at the sight of otherworldly fish. And you wonder how you lived so long before you made the choice to dive.

I remember a scuba trip I took several years ago to the British West Indies. I found a ridiculously inexpensive trip and decided to go spend some time with God's fish. The island was rustic and so was the hotel. We're talking bare-bones basic: frigid showers, mediocre food, less than luxurious rooms, and more than obnoxious smells. But the life underwater was more beautiful than anything I'd ever seen, and it made me realize just how much of God's incredible creativity we miss by staying dry and on the shore. I think He's asking us to dive right in.

And so I did. I dove into the life on that island. The fellow tourists on the trip were always complaining. One day, while running on the beach, I heard a couple arguing. The young lady was counting the curses of that underdeveloped island. It wasn't at all like what she'd read about in the brochure. (Oh, how much that trip resembled life!)

"There aren't any clubs, and we're stuck eating this hideous food in the same stupid restaurant. I'm sick of taking cold showers. I hate it here, Todd."

I stopped running and ran back to the couple. To this day, I don't know what made me do this in public on the beach, but without introducing myself, I looked at them and made this little speech:

"You know, you guys can spend the five remaining days here listing all the inconveniences and flaws. You can do this until you wear out your jaws. But the simple fact is that there isn't another plane out of here until next week. On the other hand, you could look past the shortcomings and embrace the fact that you are on a nearly deserted island. There is no tourist junk, and you can walk for miles on pure white sand. And if you'd just dive in to the crazy crystal blue, you'd see some of the most spectacular sights on the planet. You have the choice to be miserable or embrace this budget paradise." Then I smiled, thanked them for their time, and took off running again.

Days later I heard them laughing and talking at dinner. I walked up behind them and in a fake island accent asked them if everything was okay. They turned, smiling and nodding, commenting on how good everything was. Then they realized that it was me and not a waiter.

"Who in the world *are* you?" Todd asked.

"Are you a tour guide?" asked Greta, his girlfriend. "Everyone on this island seems to know you, and you seem to want everyone to have an incredibly good time. Is your job on the line?"

"I'm not a tour guide," I assured them. "I'm just a guy doing some diving and enjoying all the beauty God has made. That includes His sons and daughters. Forgive me...my name is James."

A day or so later I saw Todd and Greta walking down the beach. I ran toward them and tackled Todd in the sand. They both looked dazed, confused, and tanned. We all laughed at the absurdity of my unprovoked attack. Then I invited them to my room to have coconut-pineapple smoothies while we watched the sun set over the sea.

They came, albeit a bit reluctantly, and later they admitted that they had been a bit nervous about my intentions. When you really love people and let it flow through you unchecked, you have to expect a bit of skepticism. Love (without strings attached) really isn't all that common anymore.

While the sun set and we talked, I told them just a bit about my quest to know a most amazing God. It wasn't my intention, but I so often have to mention Him because He's such an integral part of my life.

"Out of the overflow of the heart the mouth speaks."

WWW.MATTHEW@12.34.NET

A few minutes later, we all hugged and said goodnight. A friendship had been born on that slipshod island getaway. Todd and Greta invited me to visit them after we returned to the States. I did. On one of the weekends I stayed with them, I invited them both to a Sunday morning service. (They had taken me to a concert the night before.) They hadn't been to a church where people clap and raise their hands and sing like they mean it. Greta ran out of the service crying. Confused by what she saw, she said that she couldn't get past the unusual display. It was a mild, mild sort of church— trust me—but it was more than Greta had bargained for, and we left early that day.

But over dinners, time, and a whole lot of God-love, these two lovers fell in love with the Creator of love. They began a journey beyond belief. The only problem was that they were living together. Most God-fearing Christians would have pointed that out to them before they even finished the sinner's prayer, but God challenged me to keep my mouth shut. He said He would take care of the sin; I was just supposed to love.

ANOTHER A.D.D. MOMENT

Recently, while I was driving through the High Desert, God interrupted my thoughts. He said quite clearly, *If you get the chance, let everyone you meet know this: I'm so sick of hearing "love the sinner; hate the sin." Your job is to love and let Me take care of the sin. You do your job, because I already did Mine.*

Months passed. Todd and Greta grew in grace, and in their desire to know God they came to a place where they realized that it was time to move into separate living quarters. I remember the night they called me to say, "We still love each other very much, but we want to honor God, and after praying and reading His Word, we realized that it isn't right for us to continue living this way." To say the least, I was amazed.

Less than a year later, they called me again, this time to ask me to be the best man at their wedding. I worked on the speech for days and days. It was the greatest honor, and I'll never forget how these two former castaways used their wedding to point those who attended to the God who had helped them mend the errors of their ways.

OH, TO SEE THE WONDERS THAT GOD CAN DO—IF WE ONLY DIVE INTO HIS GREAT CRYSTAL BLUE.

I believe that God wants us to dive right into unsuspecting lives to bring love, hope, and an abundance of life. However He calls us to do it, we are to be bold witnesses to all the nations, and if we listen and move in love, we'll see His net filled to overflowing. The fishing trip gets exciting when we are willing to just get going.

AN INTERESTING ASIDE:

Years and years later, after Todd and Greta were out making disciples themselves, they called to ask me a very strange question:

"James, we were talking last night, and for the life of us, there's one thing we can't figure out: Why didn't you say anything to us about our living situation when we first decided to believe?"

I thought for a moment that they might be chastising me for my lack of good judgment. But before I could defend myself, Greta said, "If you had, we would have run from you and your God. We wouldn't have wanted anything to do with Christianity or your friendship. But you moved in wisdom and let God handle it. How did you manage to keep your mouth shut?"

A mini A.D.D. MOMENT

[Very few people *ever* ask me that question. They have no reason to.]

"I know what you mean." I laughed. "But God made it very clear that I was just to love you and allow Him to lead you. He was more concerned about me doing my job and allowing Him to do His."

"The irony," Greta continued, "is that we are currently talking about Jesus with this young couple who is living together, and every single time we meet with them, we have to bite our tongues because we feel that it's our moral responsibility to point out their sin."

We laughed for a long time about our ongoing battle with religion and our need to take control. The moral of this immoral tale, it seems, is simply to let go and love the sinner while God takes care of the sin. I know there are times when it's necessary to point out some things, but it's more important to allow God to tell you when.

I don't think I can stress it enough: This fishing for men is all about love.

LOVE, LOVE, LOVE.

Sorry, I didn't mean to shout.

But it's all about hearing God—and letting Him lead in every single situation. If you make yourself available and allow Him to fill you with His love and compassion for all form and fashion of His great creation, you'll be witnesses to all nations. When you're fishing for men, just bait your hook with love—and wait.

LOVE THE SINNER, ~~HATE THE SIN~~

A FISH STORY

TIME TO FISH

WEIGHT AND SEE WHAT GOD WILL DO...

IT HAS EVERYTHING TO DO WITH THE HOLY SPIRIT
AND SO LITTLE TO DO WITH YOU.

I think the reason I don't really enjoy fishing is that it takes a lot of time and patience. However, after seeing *A River Runs Through It,* I was certain that with profishional training, I'd be great at fly-fishing. There's constant activity and an element of hunting involved. I mean, you don't have to wait for the stupid fish to bite; you try to hit the fish with the hook, right?

Anyway, back to me. There was something very romantic about the whole idea of me standing in the middle of a gorgeous river, rhythmically casting my fishing rod, waving it in slow motion through the air. I'd hear that cool little sound effect *(whoosh)* every time the rod bent over my head.

FANTASY FADES AS WE FAST FORWARD INTO REEL TIME

And the camera reveals: Me. Shivering in the obscenely cold arctic mountain stream, hip boots filling quickly with spring glacial runoff.

The actual playing out of my little fishing fantasy would include a slightly different sort of whooshing sound effect—the rhythmic thumping sort of whoosh of a medivac helicopter overhead, lowering teams of paramedics yelling at me to look up and grab the rescue hook. But I can't hear them over my own screams, "I can't see! I can't see! A fish hook's lodged in my retina!"

There are some sports I know I'm just not cut out to do. Along with my wild imagination and lack of patience, my A.D.D. would make fly-fishing an extreme sport for me. But Jesus said that, A.D.D or not, we're to be fishers of men. I realize that they used nets to bring in their catch back then…. But I still love the picture of the guys in *A River Runs Through It* waving fly rods in the air, catching fish with finesse and the help of professional wranglers who stocked the stream during the making of the film. However you do it, fishing for men or trout takes patience.

Too often we can feel pressured by the fervor of a message that feels as though it's being preached right at us—one that reminds us that Jesus calls us to make disciples of all nations, although the last time we saw a convert was when someone tricked the fat neighbor kid into coming to vacation Bible school by telling him there would be free food. After the food settled, the sensitive kid with a penchant for stories heard one about Jesus and decided that he would happily give his heart in exchange for all the nice hot dogs he had eaten. And voilà—a convert was made. Not quite the nations but, hey, he ate enough for a family of six, so that certainly was a start.

Sometimes serving hot dogs may help—just look at all the times Jesus fed the masses while He spoke to them about eternal things—but to be effective witnesses to the nations today, I think we mainly have to be plugged in to the people in our world and exhibit honest-to-goodness love and life and light. **And then wait.** If we simply allow Jesus to flow through us and do the things He commanded us to do—love the unlovable, feed the hungry, return good for evil—we can pretty much expect to see some real and tangible results. The funny thing is this: The person you least expect may be the next Saul turned Paul.

When I was in graduate school, I worked out regularly in a gym. Two cool-looking college guys, Anthony and Curtiss, worked out there too. I wasn't sure what their deal was. They were always together and kept inviting me to go away to D.C. for the weekend to meet their parents. When I realized that they were brothers, I felt a little more comfortable about their invitation. But the thought of being trapped in the car of (almost) complete strangers for a three-hour drive, just to spend two days trapped in their parents' house, sounded only a tad bit better than a prison sentence. (I'm an only child who never really experienced this sort of family bonding thing.)

I don't know what that was about, but I avoided going home with them for months. I did invite them to my apartment on several occasions, and they invited me to theirs. We cooked meals for each other and slowly got to know one another. It was probably the most awkward beginning of a friendship I've ever had. At that time, it seemed we had almost nothing in common apart from lifting weights. But God was using this simple bridge to begin a transformation that would bring about real and lasting change.

Finally Easter weekend came, and I had nowhere to go. I suppose that was because God knew I needed to go home with those guys from the gym.

When we got to D.C., we quickly said hello to their incredibly hospitable parents, and then they whisked me out to clubs where they loved to dance and stay out late. I had a good time, but I felt strangely out of place. It seemed, however, that that was the place where God wanted me to shine.

On Sunday, the family roused us from our two hours of sleep to take us to a sunrise Catholic Mass. (Well, I guess the sun didn't really rise at ten, but it felt like it should have.) I remember riding with their German grandmother, Oma. She careened wildly from lane to lane as she told me with great gusto the story of her life in Germany before she came to the States. When she turned her attention back to the road, she suddenly realized that we were flying headlong into an oncoming car. I will never forget her scream: "JEEEESUS, TAKE THE VEEEL!"

I remember screaming back, "You keep the wheel, Oma, and let Jesus handle the rest!" She did and He did. We made it safely to the Mass.

After the service, Oma pulled me aside. "You are a Spirit-filled Christian, aren't you, young man?" she asked in a loud stage whisper. (I was certain my friends were listening in.) "I know you are. I can see it in your eyes."

At that time I wasn't very comfortable with Christian labels and sometimes wasn't sure which spirit was filling me; but I did believe, and I was trying desperately to know God. So I replied, "Yes, I am."

Her smile nearly filled the church. "I've been praying for my grandbabies for many years, asking that Jesus vould send a Christian to befriend them. You are an answer to those years of prayer. Do you know that?"

Suddenly this strange trip to meet the family was making a whole lot more sense. Although it was nearly twelve years ago, I remember every detail as if it were yesterday: the food, the laughter, the strangeness of waking up to an Easter brunch with a bunch of people I barely knew but somehow knew would be closer than anyone I'd ever known.

IN TIME.

Months and months passed. I became very good friends with Anthony and Curtiss. In fact, I traveled all around Europe with Anthony, and he soon became one of my very best friends. But I never tried to force Jesus on him. I simply began to love him.

AN A.D.D. MATRIMONIAL MOMENT

While Anthony and I were still just somewhat more than acquaintances, he invited me to attend his wedding. The night before the big ceremony, one of his groomsmen became deathly ill. In a panic, the family decided that there was an extra tux they had to fill, and since I was the only one it fit, I was to be the guy who would pinch-hit—my very first role as a groomsman stunt double. At the time, it made almost no sense. But all these years later, as Anthony's best friend, seeing myself in his wedding pictures makes a whole lot of God-sense.

Almost two years after our friendship began, Anthony and I were driving home on Christmas Day around midnight. We had spent the day with Oma, his amazing Christian grandmother. Anthony was driving my car, and I was nodding off in the passenger seat when he turned his attention from the road to me.

"Why are you the way you are?" he asked. "You seem deeper and more concerned about others than most people I've met. You seem to love and you seem to really care. What's your deal?" If memory serves, my answer was simple and perhaps a bit uninspired. Remember, I was nearly asleep.

"I guess it may be because I'm trying to really get to know Jesus," I replied. "I'm trying to give Him my life, and I want to have a real relationship with Him. I guess that may be the difference."

Anthony's response was something on the lines of "Oh."

For the time being, that was all he wanted or needed to know. I fell asleep and he drove. If some sort of high-church council had been sitting in the backseat, they might have offered a brutal critique of my lame approach to presenting Jesus. Many people might say that I missed a grand opportunity to lead this wayward boy through a potent sinner's prayer. But I just remember feeling that Jesus was already there and that to say too much or do too much might distract from the love that had prompted my friend to ask me the question he asked that night. He didn't need to be hit with a hammer; he was already feeling the warmth of the light.

Often, we as Christians tend to forget that there is a process that goes on in hearts and lives, souls and minds. Our job may simply be to plant a seed and let God and time—

DO THE REST.

We often can rest. Because any good farmer knows (and I'm not good or a farmer, but I did grow up with a lot of them around) that once the seed is planted, certain things that only nature can do have to be done before its time to go and harvest. It's a lot like that, and sometimes the waiting can be the hardest.

But in the case of Anthony, I watched God unfold an incredible plan. Even though I wasn't necessarily where I should have been with God, I just happened to be the man that would serve as the bridge between this young, materialistic model and an encounter with a supernatural God.

The very next Easter at Mass (this time without me—God can do these things without our help sometimes) Anthony encountered Jesus, the God-man who bled for him upon a tree. He said that during that service he understood for the first time what the whole story was about. And there in the middle of the homily (I think that's the term), tears poured down his face as he asked Jesus into his heart.

Years have passed since that Easter Mass when a new man was born in a resurrection celebration in Washington, D.C. And I can boldly say in public that the most dynamic Christian man I know—who hears from God in a way most of us only dream about—is my best friend, Anthony. He and his wife, Julia, are empowered heroes of the faith. And even though he'd argue this point, his humility isn't fake. He left an exploding career as a model in New York to model Jesus to a very hurting world. And I can tell you that despite all he has given up in God's service, he has been blessed beyond belief. He has two boys (Joseph and James Alexander), and the adventures God has taken him and Julia on would make you wonder why more of us don't take this kind of crazy trip.

As a firsthand witness, I can tell you that being a witness to all nations may begin with just a simple conversation in a gym while working out with weights. And on your own fishing expedition, remember: **The REST may come while working out the WAITS.**

WWJB

WHAT WOULD JESUS BREW?

FISHING HOLES AND COFFEEHOUSES

I think it's time to confess: Among other things, I'm an addict. There's absolutely no other way to put it. There's one drug I do every single day. It's the first thing I think about when I wake up. I'm driven until I get it; I'm confused and dangerous when I don't. One of the reasons I've never been caught is because I've learned to make it at home, but that doesn't mean I haven't gone out and bought it on the streets. I'm not above that. Besides, before Starbucks came along, most of the stuff was cheap.

I don't know if it was the kooky high that hooked me back in college, or the fact that it helped keep me awake while I tried desperately to acquire more knowledge. However it happened, I'm hooked. My heart races just from the smell of freshly roasted beans. As far as I'm concerned, coffeehouses are some of the coolest places in the world, and they make amazing fishing holes.

Whenever I visit my friend Anthony in Raleigh, North Carolina, I make him sit with me for hours at a place called Cuppa Joes. There's something special about that space, and as far as people go, you won't find a more diverse group—a rainbow coalition, if you will, of modern philosophers, new-millennium beat poets, and ultra groovy freaks—all quaffing coffee while over-caffeineated hearts race and time just stands still.

Recently, Anthony shared a Cuppa Joe story with me—a passion play of sorts, unscripted but divinely inspired coffeehouse performance art. It was late one Sunday morning. Anthony and Julia had come in to Cuppa Joes dressed in oversized sweaters and funky ripped jeans and carrying their little son Joseph. While the two sipped coffee and read the *Times,* a young church couple came in, severely overdressed for a place like that, and sat down at a table near my friends. In a matter of only a few minutes, the starched young couple began talking loudly about the Resurrection. I'm guessing they were hoping to help save my Christian friends.

While this strange scene played out, little Joe became bored (as most young people tend to do during irrelevant conversations about resurrections) and wandered off into the smokers' room. The air was thick, but little Joe's curiosity pushed him into the hazy unknown, where he promptly introduced himself to nearly everyone in the room. Love just poured out of that little three-year-old, and he didn't seem to mind that most of the people he met were pagans and sexually confused. Joe just loved them all as he made his way around the room.

After a time, Anthony realized that Joseph was gone and headed into the smoke to find his son. Many of the young gay teens in the room noticed my good-looking friend and quickly lost interest in the antics of the little boy. Anthony looked past their looks and did pretty much what his son had done—he began saying hello to everyone. His words and actions were filled with a whole lot of love, and the coffeehouse kids began to soak up this affection and attention. But the room fell strangely silent when Joseph broke the spell by yelling "Daddy" as he ran recklessly into his father's arms.

Whatever attraction had been developing in that place, whatever thoughts might have filled those young minds, the sudden realization that they were basking in the love of a father for a son, and a son for a father, changed the tenor of the room. For several minutes, Anthony and Joseph continued to share their love with the wayward coffee drinkers, who suddenly couldn't drink in enough of that intoxicating brew.

Many had never seen such love between a father and son played out in a place like this, not for their benefit, but for the simple fact that it is. The love was real—even slightly surreal—and the immediate effect was quite concrete. When an innocent boy entered a smoke-filled room, looked past obvious differences and assorted sins, and lived out love, for the first time in their lives those kids saw what God had done when He sent His young Son to be the Christ.

That Son loved and gave until He had given all He had, all in an effort to point us back to our heavenly Dad. Even with mixed motives and misunderstandings about love, especially love for a father and love for a son, we all can see the divinely inspired Master plan that enables us to run recklessly into our Father's strong arms.

Meanwhile, back in the nonsmoking room, the sweet Christian couple continued their loud discussion of the Resurrection. Although I'm sometimes a bit thicker than I'd like to admit, I couldn't help but laugh at the irony. We who claim to believe (and I do give that well-dressed couple kudos for trying) often dress inappropriately for the tribe we're trying to reach. We come into their world discussing things that are irrelevant to them and give answers to questions no one seems to be asking, while preaching too loudly to those who already believe.

Yet in the very next room, a room filled with haze, confusion, and very damaged hearts, real needs were being met by an average little Joe, a little boy willing to go and love a room of lost strangers. Running bravely into the smoke and confusion, he inadvertently introduced them all to his Father's love, simply by his willingness to be where God could use him best.

Unless you become like a child, Jesus said, you will never enter the kingdom of heaven. Are you willing to love recklessly again, like a crazy little kid? Would you be willing to go out on a limb and simply love? Look what happened when Jesus did.

I WANT TO BE AN AVERAGE JOE... LOVING LIKE JESUS WHEREVER I GO....

I'm so in need of hearing this story again. Because as pious and loving as I may sound in recounting this coffeehouse miracle, it reminds me of where I need to live. Very recently, my own hideous lack of love and rejection of one of God's very special kids nearly cost me an opportunity to see God move in a supernatural way.

I was visiting some friends in Laguna, a family that has touched me in incredible ways. Just as I was about to say good-bye, a wildly flamboyant young man came bursting through their door. Verbose and melodramatic, he tried desperately to entertain, but it was clear that he was in a huge amount of pain. He had come to get some advice from my friend Cathy, the mother of all mothers and a lover of all kinds. She is the most patient, caring, and giving woman I think I've ever known. She doesn't judge, and despite what she may be thinking or feeling, she moves freely and speaks boldly about the Savior who is dying to set us free. I watched for a few minutes as she spoke to Jeremy, who listened, waiting for his turn.

When he got it, he began to spew out spiteful words of how God had left him burned. I stood with my arms crossed, not feeling anything like love at all, when suddenly I heard that tiny voice call me back to the place where I could go and embrace that young man in so much pain and so much need. He told me to look past the things that made me uncomfortable and get comfortable in the love that the Father had for this boy—to become like little Joseph and run recklessly into a room that smelled of smoke and heartache. *Look with My eyes, feel with My heart, and ask if you can pray.*

I did, and Jeremy replied, "Yeah, go ahead. That would be great."

So I sidled right next to him on that aptly named little love seat and asked that God's love would enable me to pray with the authority and strength that would make a difference in his broken life. I placed my hand directly on his aching heart and immediately felt a strange sensation rush through my body. There in that single touch I felt two distinct things: the pain of that boy's damaged heart and the pain of his Father who understood and even knew who and what did the breaking—the Father whose heart was also broken because of the path this boy had chosen.

I breathed deeply as the words began to form. Before I could say much at all, God's love came over me like an unexpected storm, and suddenly I could barely speak. Hot God-tears poured down my cheeks. Within seconds tears also formed in Jeremy's eyes. He sobbed uncontrollably as the love of his Father broke through the lies—the lies of rejection and abandonment that had deluged his early life, the lies that had set a poor, broken boy on a course of sheer disaster. The external voices that had ridiculed him had become his own, and the downward spiral was about to take him under. Yet all he really needed was to encounter the love of his Father and the truth of who he could be, so I held him sobbing in my arms for what seemed an eternity.

My shirt was soaked from the mingling of our tears. Those tears passed through the fabric, moved through my skin, and made their way to the hard walls around my heart. Something softened around that hard-packed shell that hadn't allowed me to love Jeremy well when I'd first seen that flamboyant young man.

God worked past the external and honored a request that was greater than my sin of rejection, the very thing that had already been killing this man. He let me act out His love in a way that ushered in real love as this boy held on to me for dear life. I wouldn't let go…and I realized that Jeremy was now looking through me into the tearful eyes of his Father while he felt His embrace. He was looking past the me that had turned away and nearly cast him aside and was seeing the real and tangible love of a Father who so often cries.

He does, you know.

The love of the Father, as it poured through me into that hurting young man, began a change in me that I pray will never go away, because I need to live forever in that land. Love will cover a multitude of sins, including rejection, abandonment, and all the other things that leave us wounded and bleeding alongside of the road. We need to act like we believe that so we can move in power wherever we go. We need to move past our fear and hold on to the broken with all our might. And in the holding of the broken we will impart the Father's life.

> There is no fear in love, but perfect love casts out fear.
>
> WWW.1JOHN@4.18.NET/NKJV

WHAT WOULD JESUS DO?

I think He'd probably be hanging out with junkies like me in a coffeehouse called Holy Grounds somewhere in the Middle East. He'd be fishing for the broken in unique watering holes, and He'd just let go and serve a triple, nonfat, whole latte love. You can bet He wouldn't judge.

And those He embraced would see past His face into the eyes of the Father of life, who would welcome them and invite them to dance around the great fire circle of the worldWide tribe.

DANCING WITH THE DREAMERS IN MY TRIBE

WHY DO WE DREAM OF THE PRIMITIVE AND FAR, WHEN THERE'S SO MUCH PAIN RIGHT WHERE WE ARE?

As God's electric fingers paint in vivid lightning strikes on the canvas of the earth's blackest skies, you make your way through the undergrowth of the Balinese jungle with calculated and well-placed steps, moving in rhythm to the beating of the drums. Under an autumnal moon, the flicker of the fire in the near distance makes for a primitive laser show of dancing long shadows. Drawing closer, you can hear the stories told in hushed tones around the glow of the fire circle.

IN MY TRIBE. IN MY DREAMS.

I dream of Indonesian excursions on small boats that ferry me through the hazards and pitfalls of the pirated Spice Islands. I think maybe I'll find an uncharted hideaway of tribes that have never heard the message that will set them free from the chains of oppression and fear-fraught destinies. Maybe something in the mystery of that grand archipelago will stir within me when I see a fantastic display of dancing, chanting, and mystifying tribal ways. Perhaps it will be there in the dance of the long shadows cast by the fire circle that I'll rise up and become emboldened by a power from on high to do things I'd never dream of doing in my neighborhood, a strip mall, or in a nearby high-rise.

In recent days I've been feeling prompted to pack up my things and journey to Jakarta to live out the picture I've just painted. I've even spent time on the Internet looking at cheap bungalows near the beach and checking out airfares, planning an adventure to a place where I've always dreamed of going to help those poor non-English speakers find a Father who loves them and a Savior who cares. And I can do it all for under two grand a month.

Then it hit me. I can do that here. I could, that is, if it weren't for the mountains of fear that keep me running past my poor English-speaking neighbors, saying a breezy hello and promising dinner sometime soon. But I always have somewhere more important to go and, unfortunately, I always seem to be late. What is causing me to live like this—propelled by some dark force that keeps me missing what's important while moving constantly in haste?

In *God.com* I suggested that God would flip our lives upside down if we would just slow down, turn things off, and begin to listen for His voice. I claimed that if we listened and believed, God would in fact speak. This is a claim that I am fairly comfortable making, because over and over again in the Bible there are direct and indirect references to God speaking to His children. This sort of God-interruption was almost as common as breathing, yet I've done radio interviews in which the hosts must have said twenty-five times in less than an hour: "Honest, this man is not nuts; he's published by Multnomah." Thirty minutes of this sort of reassurance can make you wonder about yourself.

Crazy or not, I don't believe that God speaks through our thoughts or dreams, or even through His authoritative Word, in order to make us feel good or holy or closer to Him than the next guy feels. I believe that the entire experience is also for the next guy. If we keep it to and for ourselves, I think there will come a time when God will probably become much less talkative.

I believe that God is teaching us to know His voice so we can begin to hear for those who don't even believe He exists. If you're able to hear from Him on their behalf and share some things you could never have known unless God Himself had shown you, you'll be surprised at the way this sort of listening and communication can break through even the hardest heart.

3-WAY CALLING.

It really is quite simple. Fishing can be easy when you break it all down. God will give you words to speak that are fresh baked for each person you meet, even if it's your first encounter. All you need to do is ask. When you think you've heard something from God, even if it's a picture or image in your mind's eye, or maybe just a dream, don't be afraid to step out in faith and let that person know what God has placed on your heart. Time after time God has shown up to speak through me when I was willing to step out of my pride and unbelief and into His amazing care in order to share—Jesus.

You don't have to give up all the things you do. Many of the things that make you unique are going to be the things that serve as bridges to the people you meet. God doesn't ask us to give up the things that make our lives interesting and great—unless those things bring death or rob us of His grace. God is a compassionate Father, and He wants us to live an adventure full and rich and free. And if we do this right by living out of His light, there will be so many who will see—Jesus.

If we live like we mean it.

When we do, we'll find some other unusual phenomena on this journey with a very unpredictable God. Quite frankly, if you sign up for His service, you may find that some of His requests are very odd.

FULL FRONTAL LUNACY.

Isaiah, for instance, must have cringed when God gave him

marching orders to parade around in the nude, not for just a few embarrassing minutes, but for three entire years. Jeremiah was another great prophet with an interesting assignment. He was to lounge publicly in his underwear for days on end and cook his food on human excrement. Not surprisingly, he found this most distasteful, so God, being grace full, relented and allowed him to cook his meals over fires in more conventional pits.

HOLYCOW(PIES)!

God is not an easy one to figure out. If, like these prophets of old, you are willing to move out to where the rubber meets the road and take God's message to the people who really need to hear it, you may be surprised by the things He will have you do or say so they'll be sure to hear it.

Eternity in Their Hearts is a powerful book written many years ago, one I wish every believer and fisher of men would read. In it, Don Richardson tells story after story of how successful missionaries have been when, instead of preaching to an unfamiliar people, they listen to them. They listen to their language, their stories, and their lore to see what there is in their culture that will lead them to God's front door. These missionaries have learned that by taking a tiny bit of extra time to learn what's important to a tribe, the time it takes to point them back to their Creator is reduced about a thousand times.

The point is simply that God so loved the world that He wrote His plan and message on the tablets of the heart of man. Richardson gives case histories of tribes all over the world that knew about the one true Creator before they ever encountered a missionary or messenger from God. They already had much of the information they needed; they just needed someone to help them open their eyes. They knew the truth when they heard it because it resonated deep within—reminding them of what they had once known but had forgotten.

> He has made everything beautiful in its time. He has also set eternity in the hearts of men; yet they cannot fathom what God has done from beginning to end.
>
> WWW.ECCLESIASTES@3.11.NET

I have read that book over and over again, and every time I do, I see the tribes in the world and the tribes in my neighborhood with a set of brand-new eyes. When we meet the lost, we tend to do too much talking too soon, while we should just become friends and listen. If we would take the time to find out the questions that interest them the most before trying to give them the answers, we would learn some very valuable lessons about the people we should be trying so hard to reach.

My friend David Pierce has taught me some incredibly important things about reaching out in love to introduce Jesus to tribes and peoples all around the world. David is the lead singer in an ever-changing band called No Longer Music. Although he is not really a musician, he became one when he realized something very important about the global youth culture he was trying to reach:

LEARN THE LANGUAGE BEFORE YOU SPEAK.

David asked God to give him love for the kids who have been marginalized—kids who've known heaps and heaps of pain. Contrary to popular opinion, these kids aren't the fringe; they've become the majority. They're the "in." They're tomorrow's leaders, and if we let them slip through the cracks of their own shattered hearts, we're in for a very bleak future. Research has shown that of all who claim to believe today, more than 90 percent committed their lives to Jesus before they turned eighteen. Based on what I've seen worldwide, in terms of overall effort it's almost obscene how few resources we've allocated to bring a relevant message of hope to more than one-half of the world's population—this tribe that speaks the same language. That's why David chose music as his weapon of choice, despite, shall I say, his "interesting" voice. He realized that music was the universal drumbeat behind the hearts and souls of the souls he loves to reach.

David taught me something else. Don't approach the tribe you're trying to reach with all the answers until you've taken the time to ask a whole lot of questions. He showed me the importance of a simple investment: time.

I wish all of you could meet David, or at least see some of the paths he has forged. I don't know of many men who have trusted God more. He has played in terrorist clubs in Amsterdam and places I can't even pronounce, and he even raised his sons in the red-light district, where he had to teach them not only to look both ways before they crossed the street, but also to watch for AIDS-tainted needles that could stick into their feet.

Others that I know and love are on a powerful journey beyond belief. Chris Falson makes frequent trips to Switzerland to play in nightclubs, pubs, and brothels, ministering through God-music to an audience that would never step foot inside a traditional church. So Chris and the guys just take Jesus with them and turn wherever they are into a church.

Chris moves powerfully and confidently in the Spirit as he intentionally takes time at each concert to build a concerted bridge. He plays Beatles and Zeppelin and whatever else crosses his mind to help the listeners cross the "God-bridge." By the time

Chris segues into his inspired worship music, the audience is already on board, and it isn't long before these music fans are being moved mightily by the Lord. And they have no idea when or how it hit them.

Watching David and Chris move in faith and power fueled by the love of the Father makes my own journey look rather weak. But the beauty of our God and Maker is that He has made us all unique. My calling is bound to be different if I have a different tribe to reach. It would be futile for me to try to become someone I'm not to take God's message to a group I haven't been called to reach. This is not a canvassing call for all of us to head to the nearest strip bar to take Jesus at His word to feed the hungry and clothe the naked. That kind of assumption can be quite dangerous. All I'm suggesting is that we all ask our Father where He would have us take the message of His Son. How can we show the ones who need it most the incredible things that God has done?

While living in New Zealand, I got one of those outrageous assignments from God. (Although I got to keep my clothes on and cooked my food poop-free, my mission was surprisingly odd, even to me.) I don't suggest that you try to duplicate this or make it part of your youth program. It was just a strange event that happened to me, maybe just so I could see how God can redeem any occasion and every location if we are only willing to step out and believe—or maybe step out and dance, whatever the case may be.

While working in New Zealand, in the days before things became so difficult, we had a planning meeting for our television program. Graham was in high spirits and had invited an outrageous Maori woman to meet us. Marie walked into the boardroom and let out a booming hello and some sort of interesting native Maori greeting.

I think I sat in shock through most of her discussion. She told us about the many nights she and her friends, mostly her age, would go out late to the dance clubs and raves and sit on the sidelines praying that God's Spirit would permeate the atmosphere. Marie went on to describe how they would go to the wildest underground clubs, the places where all the best DJs would spin late into the night and she and her friends would show up for a fight (in the spirit realm).

Now if you are at all like me, you are probably rolling your eyes. The thought of this being played out in some hip underground club made me wonder about this woman's sanity. But then she dropped the bomb. She said that one night God had her get out on the dance floor and begin to dance as worship unto Him. With that, I have to admit that I thought she must be "a nutter," as they say in those parts. She was about as old as my grandmother and much larger than most dancers. (What am I saying? She was larger than most dance floors!) No matter how hard I tried, I just couldn't picture any of this.

She explained how something happened that transcended age, discrimination, and simple human understanding of what can take place in the Spirit. She didn't get specific about the results of her worship in dance, but I could see in her countenance that she had tapped into something I would never understand until it became part of my experience.

Thoughts of her boldness continued to plague me. I thought about my life and how safely I'd been living. Every now and again I would venture into those clubs, and I would watch and feel out of place. Whenever I tried to dance, it quickly became clear, to me and everyone around me, that I was severely lacking in grace.

Finally, after a long, drawn-out battle with God, I decided to move outside my comfort zone and try to dance. In the past, my efforts had been only that—self-serving attempts to look good while I moved out on the floor. But now God suggested that if I would become transparent and dance as worship unto Him, His Spirit would move in and use me to point to Him.

As crazy as this sounds (and as ridiculous as it felt), I began to worship the great Creator in the most unlikely of places— The Liquor Lounge—to the mixes of trance, jungle, drum, and bass. But as I moved out in worship and stepped out in faith, something lifted me out of my rhythmically challenged self and set me in a new groove so unique that when I opened my eyes hours later, I was surrounded by about a dozen people watching me. I froze, horrified to think that I had suddenly become the center of attention. Perhaps my dancing really did stink.

But just then a wild club kid came up to me and asked, "Where did you learn that amazing groove?"

I smiled, and because I really didn't have anything else to say, I said, "God taught me the move."

She laughed and asked if I would dance with her group so they could all "vibe off my scene."

This happened time and time again. I would go into the most unlikely places and dance with reckless abandon before the God who had made me. I would dance until I was soaking wet. When I walked home through the empty, windblown streets at 5 A.M., I would feel a strange mix of adrenaline, exhaustion, and the sense that God was somehow pleased. Many nights I would have a chance to just love the kids who filled those clubs, and, on occasion, I would find that the time was appropriate to give God a great big plug.

Truth be told, I began to love to dance. And I loved the Most High God and His tribe of club kids more and more each time. Whatever that was—and it may not be for everyone, everywhere—

I learned to give myself over to the God of the universe and honor Him with my whole self.

God honored my worship by giving me a gift—an ability to dance in a way that captured the imagination of even the wildest ravers. It was effective because my purpose wasn't to preach to the club kids to make myself feel good about my quota for the lost. It was simply to go out and bring the love that Jesus brought when He hung up on the cross. My motive had to be that I cared and loved and was willing to risk and go and move to the beat that moved these kids.

Dance was a sacred thing in their economy, and the simple fact that I cared enough to learn their dance gave me license to love and permission to speak. They were tired of Christians who were irrelevant, complacent, and weak. They needed to meet the real Jesus, who would not be afraid to frequent the most outrageous clubs in an attempt to point them to the Father they desperately needed to know—the Father who is so full of love.

There is a huge lesson in all of this: Unless we take the time to learn what is sacred to the tribe we're trying to reach, and until we learn to honor them and respect that thing and find a way to honor God and bridge that gap, it will take many more years than necessary to communicate the greatest message that tribe will ever come to hear.

Don Richardson makes that perfectly clear in his incredible book. In writing eternity into the hearts of all the tribes on earth, God created a fragile spider web that connects all peoples to the heart of the Father God. If we are careful not to come in with bulldozers and heavy machinery of doctrines and agendas, we may be able to find that silvery strand.

No, I'll just preach louder if they don't understand.

If we are gentle and patient, we can point them to their own bridge, built by the God of the universe, walk with them across the gulf of sin that separates all men from the holiness of God, and introduce them to their loving Father.

Are you ready to learn to dance? If not, are you ready to listen to the music that swells up around you? It's the rhythm of the people as they dance in the pale moonlight of their own private jungles, urban or otherwise. If you really begin to listen, you'll hear more than the music. You'll begin to hear the cries and the questions, the hopes and the fears, and the oral traditions that will serve as a bridge to the Father we share.

There may even be a strange side effect. You may find that the music will move you. Whether you dance or not, moving to music by any other name is still dancing, no matter what your particular doctrine may allow. And as the music moves you, begin to move toward the ones that need you the most. Because you will quickly learn that they are the ones you need as well. In that sacred dance, hearts will be joined—yours to theirs, theirs to His, and ours to one another.

AND THE DANCE
IS THE THING
THAT PLEASES
THE KING.

THE REST

Praise be to the Lord, who has given rest to his people Israel just as He promised. Not one word has failed of all the good promises He gave.

WWW.1KINGS@8.56.NET

WHERE ARE YOU NOW?

WAITING BETWEEN THE WAVES...

I've made it to the ocean. Dry sands of the arduous desert have given way to the damp sands of the sea, and I've just come in from walking the crashing shore. My feet are still wet, and the sand is a pleasant irritant between my toes. The violence of the deafening waves has given way to a lulling sense of peace, perhaps because today I have decided once again that I really do believe.

Lord, help my unbelief.

This has been a long desert journey. Nothing about writing this book has been at all like writing *God.com*. That was an unequaled experience of extreme intimacy with a most interactive God; this desert journal has often made me wonder, many times in many ways, if that God was a figment of my imagination or if I was in some way crazed.

MY GOD, WHY HAVE YOU FORSAKEN ME?

Desert journeys are times of testing. Do we really live what we believe? It's easy to love, give, and even turn the other cheek when you are blessed and have no needs. But when the God who once spoke freely seems to have decided not to speak, and the rug feels pulled from under you and you can barely stay on your feet, it's so much harder to believe. That's the whole point of testing: to help us grow stronger and believe past what we can see.

At times I couldn't see or hear anything at all, and I had to learn to read the wind. Other times, I realized that I was right back where I'd started and would have to CHOOSE to begin again. (But remember: He forgives us when we sin.) Now I've made it to the ocean, and standing here looking out at the vastness of the sea, it's so much harder to doubt and choose to live in abject unbelief.

O GOD, I THINK I SEE.

"A lot happened before you were born," a friend used to tell me when my self-centered self-importance reared its ugly head. (He said it often.) I'm reminded of that in the presence of something so big, so powerful, and so uncontrollable as this great body of water. Walking this neither-this-nor-that parcel of dampened sand, I realized that I too am in a liminal state of softness, a place of transition where God can better mold me with His hand. I'm not ocean, and I'm not land. I'm just a stretch of His great creation, and I'm learning how to stand. He's my Father, and I'm learning to become His son.

I have some serious fears right now. A very good friend is wrestling dangerously with unbelief. I don't know where my next paycheck will come from, and I wasn't sure if this book would make it to the deadline on time or in one piece.

ONE PEACE.

I don't know what tomorrow will hold for you or me, but I do know that the great Father who holds us both controls His crashing sea. Something in the ocean brought me hope today as I walked and talked with my invisible Friend of friends. I think it may have been the comfort of knowing that so much is going on under the direction of a hand I cannot see.

I made the sand a boundary for the sea, an everlasting barrier it cannot cross. The waves may roll, but they cannot prevail; they may roar but they cannot cross it.

WWW.JEREMIAH@5.22.NET

Whether God speaks or not, His existence is clearly evident in everything I see, and today He gently reminded me that I am in control of almost nothing at all. I can only choose to trust Him and acknowledge the truth that I am frail and embarrassingly small. Only God through His own strength and power will enable me to fulfill His call.

And He will, you know—if I continue on this journey called believe.

He who has begun a good work is faithful to complete it.

WWW.1THESSALONIANS@5.24.NET

So as I walked that transitional body between the unknown depths of the sea and the firmness of dry land, I made a powerful commitment: I'm going to stay soft while I allow Him to mold me as I rest in the hollow of His hand.

My God has made some bold promises. I haven't seen them all come to pass, but I can rehearse the miracles I've seen so far, and I can live by the sea and cast. And as I cast, God will fill my net, sometimes with fish, sometimes with faith, and sometimes with the love of friends. And friends will sometimes be my net, depending on where I am.

I'm learning to wait and trust. And when the catch seems less than I might expect, I'll remind myself that in the grand scheme of things, I've really seen nothing yet. I'll keep listening for the voice of the greatest fisherman of all, and He will tell me when to take the next trip and where to cast my net. He will also help me know when it's just time to sit and rest while waiting out a squall.

Walking on the shore or resting in the sand, I'm going to dance as worship whenever I possibly can, because the dance is the thing that pleases the King. Look at David—he's the man. Our God loves worship in all its forms—in music, dance, and poetry. He takes pleasure in worship that flows from our living—worship that says clearly, "Lord, I really do believe. And it doesn't depend upon what I see."

I'm going to live in that place of unsafe safety and dance wildly on God's high wire, knowing that no matter how high we swing on His grand trapeze, His net is there to break our fall. The net offers a real sense of peace, and a fall never, ever means defeat. It means you were bold enough to try and bold enough to believe. And as you swing wildly with the crowd screaming down below, remember that there's another crowd—a cloud of witnesses from long ago—that has gone before you. They too weathered many deserts, tests, and falls, and through them they learned on whom to call.

> These all died in faith, not having received the promises,
> but having seen them afar off were assured of them,
> embraced them and confessed that they were strangers and pilgrims
> on the earth.… But now they desire a better, that is,
> a heavenly country. Therefore God is not ashamed
> to be called their God, for He has prepared a city for them.
> WWW.HEBREWS@11.13–16.NET/NKJV

I'm going to reach that city one day and meet that great cloud of witnesses—those fathers and mothers of faith. And I don't want to ever give up, ever lose hope, or ever give in to my fears. I want to feel their welcoming embrace.

But today I just want to rest here at the ocean, believing beyond what I can see. God's authoritative Word says that I can enter His rest when I live in a land called **believe.** That's what heaven is—a place of rest for those who are bold enough to take the journey beyond belief. Fear, doubt, anxiety, jealousy, striving, and wrath are all by-products of unbelief. But when we let all that go and trust with our soul, we can rest in the hollow of His hand. We can dwell in the secret place of the Most High God, in the sea, in the sky, or in any land.

Wherever we live, our job as His sons and daughters is to choose to believe and be willing to move out in trust. Are you willing to step out of the fake into real faith and ask God to give you His power from on high? Will you ask for more of His love so you can rise above the futility of living safe and high and dry? Will you embrace a community of believers who will surround you like a net? Will you live in fearless confidence that our God hasn't failed you yet? Will you learn with me, as I learn to let go in a place of trust and rest?

OUR FATHER DESIRES ONLY THE BEST.

I'm at the ocean now. I'm watching the surfers bob carefree in the waves. Even though the pounding surf makes it impossible to hear what they say, they're teaching me an important lesson about the journey beyond belief. Surfing is a lot like catching His Spirit—riding on the crest of love and power fueled by grace—but no matter how good we become or how great our technique, we can never make the waves.

Only God does that.

We must simply REST while we wait.

REST.
AND WAIT
EXPECTANTLY
BETWEEN THE
WAVES.

They will feast on the abundance of the seas, on the treasures hidden in the sand."

WWW.DEUTERONOMY@33.19.NET

WHERE ARE YOU NOW?

Gather with us around the flickering fire circle of the worldWide
web and share your story with the members of our tribe.

WWW.THEREST.NET

The publisher and author would love to
hear your comments about this book. *Please
contact us at:* www.multnomah.net/godnet

GET ON-LINE WITH THE CREATOR

God.com offers a refreshing, unflinchingly honest approach to connecting with our Creator. In these pages, author James Langteaux boldy tackles some of our toughest questions about maintaining a relationship with an invisible being—discussing God as Father, Lover, and Best Friend. *God.com* helps us identify and break down walls of fear so we can allow God's love and purposes to change our lives in profound ways.

ISBN 1-57673-707-1

"INNOCENT, POIGNANT, AND PROFOUND!"

—PHIL JOEL, NEWSBOYS